THE HEIDELBERG
CATECHISM

A New Translation
for the
Twenty-first Century

———

Translated by Lee C. Barrett III
With an Introduction

The Pilgrim Press
Cleveland

To my mother and the memory of my father, who taught me the essentials of the faith.

The Pilgrim Press
700 Prospect Avenue
Cleveland, Ohio 44115-1100
thepilgrimpress.com

11 10 09 08 07   5 4 3 2 1

Library of Congress Cataloging-in-Publication Data

Heidelberger Katechismus. English. 2007
    The Heidelberg Catechism : a new translation for the 21st century / translated by Lee C. Barrett III ; with an introduction. — 1st ed.
        p. cm.
    Includes bibliographical references.
    ISBN 978-0-8298-1762-1 (alk. paper)
1. Reformed Church—Catechisms—English. I. Title.
    BX9428.A3 2007
    238'.42—dc22   2007009928

Contents

Introduction

Catechisms and Doctrines—What Good Are They?

THE ULTIMATE IDENTITY of any religious body lies in its basic convictions—that is, its core beliefs about God, the universe, and human life. Communities of faith attract and hold human hearts and minds because they offer answers to life's most enduring questions: Where do we come from? Why are we here? What can we hope for? Churches remain vital and vibrant only as long as they can offer compelling "good news" to people who suffer from a deep dissatisfaction with their own moral lives, who hunger for justice in the face of exploitation, who long for a sense of meaning and significance, and who are burdened by tragedies and griefs. The theological heritage of the family of denominations rooted in the Swiss and western German Reformations (often called the "Reformed" tradition) does indeed address these issues in powerful and comprehensive ways. According to our heritage, we are first and foremost a community that believes itself to be called into existence to adore the glorious maker of heaven and earth, to receive and celebrate God's reconciling grace, and to respond to God's call to love and to serve. These convictions, rather than our polity or programs, most basically define who we are. These foundational beliefs about God, God's universe, and our place in that universe motivate and sustain our concerns for worldwide justice, joyful evangelism, extravagant hospitality, self-giving compassion, and generous ecumenism.

The pressures of contemporary life pull even devout congregants in so many divergent directions that the basic contours of their identity as Christians is often obscured. A unique feature of our postindustrial era is that most persons, at least in North America, are shaped by multiple communities and value systems, including the pop electronic media and the culture of consumerism. The messages of many discordant and even warring cultural voices vie for mastery in our heads. In the midst of such a cacophony of values, remembering or identifying the basic themes of the Christian faith is often difficult. In an era in which the church is competing with the entertainment industry for the minds and hearts of its people, the church may need to be increasingly vigilant so that the essential shape of its faith is not forgotten. Perhaps now more than ever, it is wise to subject to scrutiny our hodgepodge of cultural assumptions and values, in order to sort through the many conflicting claims upon our loyalties. It may also be wise to remind ourselves of our core convictions as Christians. We must try to discern which of our operative convictions actually have anything to do with our Christian heritage, and which ones spring from entirely different, and perhaps regrettable, sources. In order to accomplish the discernment, we must recover the wisdom of our ancestors in the faith. We need to know where we have come from in order to understand who we are and where we are to go. We must look back to the history of our Christian communities, to search for the basic convictions that governed their common life and informed their thinking, feeling, and acting. By ferreting out the dimly remembered continuities that link our past to our present—the continuities encoded in our historic confessional documents, particularly our catechisms—we may well uncover unexpected resources for renewal. We may discover a wealth of riches, much of it almost forgotten, that can be mined to make our contemporary experience more genuinely Christian. In short, our churches could achieve a renewed sense of identity through prayerful reflection on the core doctrines expressed in our catechisms.

Of course, words like "catechism" and "doctrine" are not popular in contemporary society. To most North Americans they suggest rigidity, authoritarianism, and the curtailment of individual freedom. This antipathy to inherited teachings is not entirely new; in fact, it is the fruit of deep-rooted histori- cal dynamics. Even in the eighteenth century, many serious Christians had begun to question the value of such confes- sional documents as catechisms, suspecting that they might be incompatible with the Reformers' supposed rejection of the medieval church's reliance upon authoritarian church tra- ditions. Extrapolating from the alleged example of Luther, they came to regard the individual's capacity to formulate his or her own beliefs, unencumbered by traditions and institu- tions, as a paramount religious right. In the United States, the political and subsequent cultural disestablishment of Christianity made the notion of authoritative teachings seem even more alien. Furthermore, the prevalent identification of faith with personal decision and interior spiritual life made it difficult to see how institutional pronouncements from remote historical periods could be meaningful to an individual. Historical criticism of the catechisms and creeds that exposed their rootage in archaic conceptualities, and the tendency to dismiss them as the products of outdated worldviews, further contributed to the distrust of tradition. More recently, the "postmodern" suspicion of all truth claims has rendered confessions and catechisms even more problematic. As alternatives, many contemporary Christians have turned to religious experience or ethical action rather than theological convictions to provide the glue that holds churches together. For example, the Universal Christian Conference on Life and Work in 1925 popularized the slogan that "service unites while doctrine divides." This "deeds over creeds" sensibility would eventually blossom in the popularity of the question "What would Jesus do?" It is no wonder that many loyal church members are inclined to reduce Christianity without remainder to moral action or vague feelings of transcendence.

Much of this hostility toward orthodox statements of faith is understandable, for all too often in our history confessional divisions have spawned conflict, bitterness, and even violence. By the late sixteenth century, the proliferation of confessions of faith more often than not sowed seeds of discord rather than concord. Protestants vilified Roman Catholic teachings, Lutherans condemned many Reformed doctrines, and everyone persecuted the Anabaptists. The confessional documents from this period were often peppered with a generous dose of anathemas aimed at rival Christian groups. Sadly, the authority of the state was often invoked to enforce doctrinal conformity and to employ violence to defeat theological alternatives. Not surprisingly, many thoughtful Christians from John Locke to John Shelby Spong have identified the concern for doctrinal integrity as a primary source of Christendom's ills.

However, an admission of the importance of "doctrines" and the catechisms that articulate them need not eventuate in these abuses. Core convictions do not necessarily generate intolerance. Nor does the willingness to attend to the testimony of a tradition necessarily spawn a slavish subservience to the authority of the past. Nor does the holding of beliefs about the nature of God and the meaning of human life necessarily detract from the strength of personal experience or the zeal of commitment to transformative action in the world

The truth is quite the contrary. The effort of many contemporary people to dispense with doctrines is futile and self-defeating. The current prevalent unhappiness with talk of doctrines is rooted in a misunderstanding concerning exactly what doctrines are and how they function. Actually, doctrines are indispensable; everyone has them, and no one can live without them. Individuals may not be able to articulate, or even know that they are harboring their doctrines. People certainly may not be able to step back from their doctrines to evaluate and critique them. Nevertheless, all of us make decisions, formulate plans, succumb to fears, and cherish hopes that are based on sweeping assessments of what the world is like, and what people are like.

To give a very mundane example, I brush my teeth because I assume that keeping one's bodily parts, including teeth, in functional order will contribute to my well-being and make life more pleasant for my associates. I also assume that such care of myself and my immediate community is an appropriate response to the gift of life that I have been given. For me, these inchoate and usually unspoken convictions function as doctrines, guiding my behavior and shaping my emotions. Insofar as we entertain beliefs about the way things most basically are, we cannot escape from holding doctrines. All of us have core convictions that function as a sort of lens through which we view the world. These core convictions, which can be called "doctrines," lead us to regard some sorts of behavior as being suited to the way things are, and other sorts of behavior as being out of alignment with reality. They also lead us to feel certain emotions rather than others, and even to harbor certain long-range hopes and fears. If the existence of ghosts is one of my doctrines, I will be inclined to experience fear in allegedly haunted houses and may devote inordinate time and energy to avoiding cemeteries. Our doctrines, even such idiosyncratic ones, thus serve for us as boundaries that demarcate appropriate feelings and responses from inappropriate ones. Consequently, doctrines are not just cognitive propositions that are dispassionately entertained by the mind; rather, they are rules that regulate the well-springs of both feeling and action.

Doctrines are the implicit principles governing communal ways of living and being. They are the rules, often so familiar and pervasive that their operation is not even noticed, that structure a community's way of life. Accordingly, doctrines have been likened to the grammatical rules of a living language that provide the very basis for combining sounds into publicly intelligible meanings.[1] They have also been compared to the rules of a game, without which the game would devolve into idiosyncratic and arbitrary behaviors.[2] In baseball, the proposition that three strikes constitute an out has the status of a doctrine; it is so integral to the playing of the game that it is taken for granted in the formulation of strategy. If an

---

1. See, for example, George Lindbeck, *The Nature of Doctrine* (Minneapolis: Fortress Press, 1984), and William Placher, *Unapologetic Theology: A Christian Voice in a Pluralistic Conversation* (Louisville, KY: Westminster/John Knox Press, 1989).

2. See Paul Holmer, *The Grammar of Faith* (San Francisco: Harper & Row, 1978).

individual player suddenly decides to reject this rule, the very integrity of the game is in jeopardy. Without such commonly held doctrines, games could not be played and communities could not function at all.

Some doctrines are absolutely foundational for a community's identity and way of life. For example, academic life is based on the assumption that divergent interpretations of phenomena should be resolved through a civil exchange of views, the citing of evidence, and the presentation of arguments rather than by violence. Academic life could not proceed without this assumption. In this way, some doctrines serve as the presupposition of everything the community does. Such doctrines as the Trinity and the incarnation have historically functioned that way for Christianity. The passing on of a community's foundational doctrines from generation to generation is absolutely critical for that community's survival.

These most central and crucial doctrines of a community are rooted in historical traditions. They do not spring up overnight, nor are they the products of passing fads. In order to function as a settled rule, a principle must be practiced for a good while, until it becomes second nature and taken for granted. For example, in Western culture the political doctrine of inalienable human rights seems intuitively plausible because it has functioned in our civil life for quite some time. To be effective, doctrines must have developed over a period of time. They must be evident in the lived history of a human community, stretching back into a community's past. Even the revision and modification of doctrines, phenomena that occur with regularity in a community's history, require the community's general perception that the novel elements are natural extensions of the trajectory of its convictions. Consequently, the effort to retrieve a community's doctrines inevitably involves an exploration of its historical heritage.

Sometimes communities find it necessary to explicitly formulate their core convictions in order to instruct members in their proper use. Most of the time, people acquire these core convictions through the internalization of the attitudes, habits, and values of the human communities that they trust or that powerfully shape them. Ordinarily this happens through a variety of informal means, such as singing certain songs, sharing certain experiences, imitating the behavior of role models, and engaging in particular projects. Although most doctrines are simply implicit in a community's life, being the way the community members ordinarily do things, sometimes doctrines need to be overtly and publicly articulated. Often this happens when a community feels perplexed, not knowing how to proceed in the face of new challenges that disturb business as usual. In such circumstances, it may seem that people have become confused about the basic "grammar" of their common life, and that some people have begun to act "ungrammatically." That perplexity and alarm often fosters reflection on the true nature of the community's basic principles in order to gain clarity about their application to new situations. For example, the gradual cultural and social empowerment of women catalyzed reflection on the nature of political rights and the explicit formulation of constitutional laws, a legal variety of doctrine. Analogously, in response to novel developments and ambiguous issues, many religions have felt the need to clarify and state the rules governing their common life. Or sometimes the need to make doctrines explicit arises because of the challenges and difficulties of introducing the faith to children and adult converts. Sometimes the informal channels of socialization are not sufficient for passing on the faith. Admittedly, some religions, like the Greco-Roman cults of the New Testament period, did not typically produce fixed and formal summaries of core convictions. But Christian faith, with its commitment to a specific God revealed in a particular heritage and through particular sacred texts, very quickly did see fit to articulate and elucidate its most central tenets. Often this was motivated by a polemical purpose, the need to oppose proposed ways of living out the faith that seemed to involve a fundamental betrayal of some of the church's most cherished values. In much the same way, the native speakers of a language may feel the need to stipulate explicit rules of grammar when some members of their population begin to speak in such divergent ways that intelligibility is endangered. In any case, Christianity has been among the religions most prone to make its implicit convictions explicit in the form of doctrinal formulations.

Our spiritual ancestors developed catechisms, creeds, and confessions because they feared that the Christian life would lose its distinctive shape unless its central themes were publicly acknowledged and affirmed. Christian faith, they knew, is not an amorphous experience that spontaneously wells up in people, but is a specific way of life with a morphology that can be described. For example, Christian hope is not just a diffuse attitude of optimism, but a much more specific expectation that God can bring reconciliation out of sin, liberation out of oppression, and life out of death. In the creeds and confessions, this definite morphology of the Christian faith was expressed as a sort of objective content, a public teaching. Consequently, a constant refrain in the treatises and sermons supporting the catechisms and creeds is that such cardinal virtues as faith, hope, love, trust, and service cannot be based on vague sentiments, passing intuitions, or misleading teachings.

When the core religious convictions are formalized in a confessional document such as a catechism, they are usually given the sanction of a relevant legitimating religious authority. Typically such crucial documents are the products of official processes designed by the churches, ideally including lengthy debate and conversation. Catechisms and creeds have most often undergone a formal or informal process of reception by the churches, analogous to the ratification of a constitutional amendment. A document like a catechism therefore possesses a certain type of communal and institutional authority. It carries more weight than does the opinion of a solitary individual relying on nothing more than his or her private experience.

Although our catechisms, creeds, and confessions were ratified by authoritative ecclesiastical bodies, they were not arbitrary impositions by authoritarian elites, as is often alleged by the pop media. Of course, one can discern political motives at work in the development of the catechisms and the other confessional documents. But, more basically, they grew out of the common life of the church as it used Scripture in its worship, moral struggles, and mission to the world. The old slogan that "the law of faith" ("*lex credendi*") follows the "law of worship" ("*lex orandi*") accurately describes the dynamics that generated the great catechisms and confessions. For example, in the early centuries of Christianity the full divinity of the Holy Spirit was affirmed largely because the church found itself experiencing a kind of empowerment that could only be from God, and honoring the Spirit with divine titles. Similarly, the formulators of the Nicene-Constantinopolitan creed argued that the Persons of the Trinity must be declared to be equal because they are equally glorified in the liturgy. Doctrines were intended to articulate the basic underlying principles already being practiced in the Christian community, similar to the way that grammarians make explicit the underlying rules implicit in the practice of language users. The doctrines were "rules" ("*regulae*") articulating the deep grammar of the Christian life.

This effort to recover our bearings by exploring our Christian doctrinal heritage expressed in documents like the Heidelberg Catechism need not lead to the dreaded stagnation that some contemporary people so deeply fear. On the contrary, the appropriation of a convictional tradition is actually a prerequisite for any novel theological insight. Without such an orientation, we would have no perspective from which to survey the contemporary scene and would certainly have nothing coherent, much less novel, to say. Admittedly, as we look to the past, we will indeed encounter language that is culturally conditioned, opinions that seem quaint or archaic, and assertions that are clearly restricted to a particular historical cultural setting. But we will also discover motifs that have the power to speak to new times and contexts. We will find surprising insights that can be adapted to new cultural environments and ultimately transform them. A doctrinal tradition is not the mechanical repetition of an immutable formula in which nothing new is ever expressed. Rather, a tradition is a historically extended conversation among the members of a community in which that community's basic convictions are continuously reformulated and renegotiated by new generations.[3] A doctrinal tradition need not and should

---

3. See Alasdair MacIntyre, *After Virtue* (Notre Dame, Ind.: University of Notre Dame Press, 1981).

not stifle all diversity of points of view. Within a tradition's trajectory there is ample freedom to explore and experiment. For example, to be Lutheran is to be convinced that the true meaning of the doctrine of justification by grace through faith is worth a lifetime of passionate debate, and that the conversation about its true import must be continued. However, not all Lutherans interpret "justification by grace" in the same way, and new possible meanings for that phrase are constantly explored. Similarly, Wesleyans continue to wrestle with the significance of "holiness" for contemporary life, and Presbyterians continue to explore what the "sovereignty of God" may mean for the twenty-first century. To participate in any tradition is to transport a theme, inherited from the ancestors, into new and sometimes contested territory.

Our efforts to learn from the theological convictions of our ancestors in the faith need not degenerate into a narrowly "heady" approach to Christianity. In spite of the emphasis on doctrine as objective teaching, the confessional documents, especially the catechisms, were not intended only to be propositions for the mind to entertain. The catechisms and confessions were just as much affairs of the will and the heart as they were of the head. For example, the first question of the Heidelberg Catechism forces the learner to face the agonizing issue of where in this uncertain and precarious life a human being can find any comfort. The themes of anxiety, trust, guilt, relief, despair, and joy run through the catechism as constant refrains. Although post–Reformation-era theologians sometimes tended to distinguish the cognitive and the more passional aspects of faith, separating faith as assent to propositions from faith as trust, earlier Christians more typically regarded belief as inseparable from passionate commitment. Affirming the confessional documents required a sincere pub-

lic act; by saying the words of the creed or by reciting the catechism's answers, an individual was taking a stand before
humanity and making a pledge to God. By repeating the
phrases of the catechism or confession, an individual was
vowing to be faithful. The affirmation of belief was not a neu-
tral declaration of ideological opinions; the act had a profound
self-involving and self-committing force. Appropriately, the
Latin word for "confession"—*confessio*—had a nuance of
thanks and praise of God, as well as a hint of accusation of
oneself. Because of this, saying a catechism in public not only
committed an individual to the cultivation of certain emotions
and passions, but itself was an emotionally charged act.

Given such a rich and complex integration of heart, will,
and mind in the act of confessing one's faith, it is not surprising that catechisms, creeds and confessions have served a
variety of practical functions in the life of the church. Some
confessional documents, the creeds, summarize the essentials
of the faith in relatively brief formulae intended for recital
during worship and other public ceremonies, while others, the
confessions, provide more exhaustive accounts intended to
guide appropriate preaching and teaching. Like all confessional documents, the catechisms were used to express norms
or at least guidelines for the churches of our ancestors in the
faith. However, the catechisms were employed most typically
for very special educational purposes. They functioned as
condensations of the basic tenets of the faith in order to
instruct and orient new members to the Christian community.
Often the catechisms were regarded as so crucial as to require
memorization by all church members. Not uncommonly they
also served as guidelines for ministers, as indicators of the
pivotal themes to be stressed in the proclamation of the
gospel, in order to ensure that preaching did not degenerate

into the broadcasting of idiosyncratic opinions and idle speculations. At times the series of topics in a catechism was even employed to structure the training of ministers. Catechisms often functioned to distinguish sound teaching from misleading or inadequate interpretations of the faith and even to polemicize against perceived heretics. In the post-Reformation Protestant world, catechisms became powerful symbols of a religious community's identity and solidarity. These multiple and divergent functions have shaped the forms and styles of the various catechisms, causing some to be terse and staccato and others to be florid and elaborate.

Catechisms had been used by Christian churches long before the Heidelberg Catechism was composed. Some were intended for children, others were aimed at adults, and yet others were designed to provide a model of instruction for teachers and pastors. By the later Middle Ages, catechetical practice typically employed the Ten Commandments, the Apostles' Creed, and the Lord's Prayer (and sometimes the Ave Maria) to focus the instruction. This basic sequence was adopted so that the law could expose the nature of the human predicament, then the creed could present the medicine that remedies that lamentable situation, and finally the prayer could teach humanity how to yearn for and appropriate this remediation. To make this arrangement even more attractive, the Ten Commandments, the Apostles' Creed, and Lord's Prayer were regarded in the Middle Ages as corresponding to the essential virtues of love, faith, and hope.

The Reformation inspired an even greater concern for theological literacy among laypeople. During his travels in Germany in 1528, Martin Luther was appalled at the widespread lack of familiarity with the basics of the Christian faith and at the failure of the clergy to adequately proclaim the gospel. His experience during his journey ultimately convinced him of the necessity to undertake the project of producing an adequate introduction to the basics of the faith himself. Accordingly, in 1529 Luther wrote a large catechism for pastors and a smaller one for the uneducated laity and for children. He retained the basic medieval structure, omitting the Ave Maria and adding sections on the sacraments and other matters. Given Protestantism's dual emphasis of the centrality of sound doctrine as well as the priesthood of all believers, the catechisms would not surprisingly become a primary genre of confessional document in order to ensure that all believers were doctrinally literate. Luther's Small Catechism became enormously popular, being distributed as large posters to be hung prominently on church walls and as illustrated booklets, and were often used as primers. But Luther's Small Catechism was not without a host of rivals. In the sixteenth century, Protestant territories commonly produced their own catechisms, suited to their own theological tastes. Much of Protestant Europe became saturated with a profusion of eclectic and idiosyncratic catechisms. The newly invented printing press contributed to this frenzy of catechism production by making it possible for laypeople to possess their own copies for use at home. By the early 1560s in the region of Heidelberg, several different catechisms, some Lutheran and some Reformed, were in circulation.

Many church leaders, including the secular lord Elector Frederick the Pious of the Palatinate, feared that this cacophony of voices would jeopardize the transmission of Christianity's central doctrines to the next generation and undermine the unity of the faith. This chaotic situation motivated the composition of one of the most enduring and influential catechisms that Christianity has seen.

The Distinctiveness of the Heidelberg Catechism

The Heidelberg Catechism of 1563 became the chief doctrinal standard of the Reformed churches of Hungary, the Netherlands, and Germany. More than any other document except the Bible, it molded and nurtured the religious experience of Reformed German Protestants in the Rhineland. In Dutch Reformed circles it was taught to young people over a period of several years in order to prepare them for church membership. Dutch pastors preached through the catechism each year, usually in a Sunday evening service, grouping the questions into fifty-two days to correspond to the weeks of the church year. From these European roots, the catechism has spread to shape the piety of Christians from Michigan to Indonesia, and from Pennsylvania to Honduras. Ever since Jacob Philip Boehm, one of the pioneers of the German Reformed Church in North America, declared adherence to the Heidelberg Catechism as his doctrinal standard and established it as a norm for his new congregations, this document has been at the core of German Reformed piety in the United States.

The catechism takes its name from the ancient city of Heidelberg on the Neckar River, the capital of the Palatinate region of Germany. The catechism was sponsored and adopted in 1563 by Elector Frederick III, the ruler of this politically important principality. The Palatinate was a dominant power in southwestern Germany (known as "upper" Germany), being one of the secular principalities that constituted the loose political unit known as the Holy Roman Empire, stretching from Austria to the Baltic Sea. The religious situation in the Palatinate was peculiar and troubling.

Lutheran influences from Saxony and neighboring Nuremberg had been felt in the 1540s, and Lutheran forms of worship were practiced rather clandestinely out of fear of antagonizing the Catholic Holy Roman Emperor, whose political influence in the area was considerable. During the 1540s and 1550s, the rulers of the Palatinate (known as "electors"), Ludwig V and Frederick II, attempted to navigate a middle course between the opposed Catholic and Protestant camps, allowing some Protestant reforms without breaking with the Roman Catholic Church and thereby offending the emperor. After the ascension of Elector Otto Henry in 1556, this situation began to change. According to the Peace of Augsburg of 1555, which terminated a series of religious wars between Catholics and Protestants in Germany, the Catholic and Lutheran faiths were recognized as acceptable religions for the empire's principalities, depending on the religious preference of the local prince. Accordingly, in 1556 the new Elector Otto Henry declared the Palatinate to be Lutheran, and announced that the Lutheran Augsburg Confession was its doctrinal norm. However, more Reformed influences from neighboring Switzerland and Strasbourg had also appeared surreptitiously, and Otto Henry himself invited not only conservative Lutherans but also followers of the Reformed theologian Ulrich Zwingli, who had been the leading theologian of Zurich, to teach in the university. These developments sowed the seeds of bitter religious controversy. The Reformed teachings, or at least the somewhat Reformed-leaning opinions of the moderate Lutheran theologian Philip Melanchthon, were favored by Frederick, Otto Henry's heir-apparent, who himself became Elector Frederick III (known as "the Pious") in 1559. This drift of the ruling house toward the Reformed end of the theological spectrum antagonized the highly orthodox Lutheran Duke Christopher of Württemberg, who complained that the Reformed faith violated the tenets of the Augsburg Confession that served as a standard for Lutheranism. This accusation was politically significant, because only the Lutheran variety of Protestantism that recognized the authority of the Augsburg Confession was included in the religious settlement of the Peace of Augsburg. Reformed theologies that deviated from the Augsburg Confession were not to be tolerated as the religion of any German principality. Consequently, Elector Frederick had to demonstrate to Emperor Maximilian II that the faith he hoped to foster was indeed congruent with the Augsburg Confession. There was some reason to be optimistic that this could be accomplished, for Maximilian was a moderate Catholic who wanted to avoid a potentially disastrous civil war. (In 1566 Maximilian at a meeting of the Imperial Diet in Augsburg did judge the Heidelberg Catechism to be within the bounds of the Augsburg Confession and confirmed Frederick as a prince of the Holy Roman Empire.)

But the Palatinate's religious problems were not merely external. Religious feuds and rivalries disrupted the domestic tranquility of the region. As we have seen, under the succession of electors a volatile mixture of divergent theological opinions had arisen in the region, with ministers who held rival views viciously condemning one another from their pulpits. Moreover, few trained Protestant ministers were available, sects proliferated, and folk traditions dominated religious life. The tension between the Lutheran and Reformed factions erupted into symbolic violence when in Heidelberg itself a high Lutheran pastor wrenched the cup of blessing from the hands of his Reformed assistant who had been raising it during the celebration of the Eucharist. The assistant favored the theology of Zwingli, whose views on the Eucharist differed sharply from Luther's conviction that Christ is mysteriously physically present in the sacrament. Frederick desperately needed something to unify the rival groups of Protestants in the Palatinate, something that would look Lutheran enough to satisfy the terms of the Peace of Augsburg but would also be acceptable to his Reformed subjects.

The situation required something that could serve both as a catechism to nurture a new generation in a common faith and as a confession to displace the multiple Lutheran and Reformed catechisms and other confessional documents that were circulating and fomenting dissension. Accordingly, Frederick enlisted the services of Zacharius Ursinus, a twenty-eight-year-old theologian at the University of Heidelberg, to participate on a team charged with developing the new catechism. Ursinus had been a student of Philip Melanchthon, the conciliatory Lutheran leader who had grown up in the Palatinate and who had also advised Frederick. Significantly, Ursinus had also been exposed to Reformed thought, making him well suited to perform a mediatorial role. Ursinus was assisted by Caspar Olevianus, a talented young preacher who had studied under John Calvin in Geneva and was familiar with Calvin's successor Theodore Beza. Although how much of the catechism Olevianus may have composed is not clear, he is probably responsible for the introduction of themes reminiscent of Beza. Following the recommendation of Melanchthon (who had died), Ursinus proposed that they strive for biblical simplicity and shun the arcane complexities of scholastic theology, a policy that gave the catechism its simple elegance. Other scholars from the university and prominent ministers seem to have functioned as part of the authorial team throughout 1562. Church superintendents and even lay leaders such as Frederick himself served as consultants and editors toward the end of the process. A Latin text of the catechism was produced for scholars, for Latin was the international language of the learned world, while a more popular German version was also prepared for general use. The catechism was officially approved by a Heidelberg synod in January 1563, and the text went through four different editions in German in 1563 alone. Given the theological orientation of its authors, it was inevitable that the catechism would combine elements of the moderate Lutheranism of Melanchthon and elements of Reformed thought. The final product approximated Frederick's goal: it focused attention on the themes that united Lutheran and Reformed churches and avoided most of the issues (except, perhaps, the Eucharist) that divided them.[4]

A certain "Lutherish" flavor is evident in the catechism. Like the Lutheran confessions, it tends to focus on the work of Christ, emphasizing God's redemptive activity. Like the Augsburg Confession, the catechism concentrates on the individual's spiritual need for reconciliation in the face of sin and for solace in the face of tragedy and insecurity. Unlike many confessions of faith and some other catechisms from this era, it does not commence with an abstract definition of God's nature and attributes. Nor is it organized according to highly theoretic ruminations concerning the sequence of God's eternal decrees of election and reprobation. The catechism is

---

4. See Lyle D. Bierma, *An Introduction to the Heidelberg Catechism: Sources, History, and Theology* (Grand Rapids: Baker Academic, 2005).

organized not according to speculative interests but rather to practical considerations. Its dialogical format follows the sequence of questions that would naturally arise in the living of the Christian life. Appropriate to this personal, existential orientation, the catechism's most famous and opening question is: "What is your only comfort, in life and in death?" The answer, echoed in different ways throughout the catechism—that "I belong, both body and soul, in life and in death, not to myself, but to my faithful savior Jesus Christ"—establishes the prevailing mood of hope and confidence. The essence of the good news is that I do not need to safeguard my own earthly or eternal security; true comfort is freely given with the knowledge that God, through Christ, has claimed me as God's own child. Accordingly, the catechism reflects the flow of Christian experience, being structured around the movement from guilt and misery to the celebration of God's grace that redeems us from that sin and misery, and on to our response of gratitude for that grace. Its basic structure has often been neatly summarized as "guilt, grace, and gratitude."

Within this very common Protestant pattern (rooted ultimately in the structure of the Epistle to the Romans and used at various times by both Lutheran and Reformed writers), more Reformed motifs, typical of the irenic heritage of Peter Martyr and Martin Bucer, are injected. For example, the catechism stresses the theme that God is sufficiently powerful to ensure that all will ultimately be well with us, although the document refuses to speculate about exactly how God's will operates in the universe to bring about this state of felicity. Also in a Reformed manner it reminds us that although Christ is indeed in solidarity with us (as the Lutherans stressed), nevertheless Christ rules with sovereign power in heaven. In its third section the catechism presents obedience as an integral part of our grateful response, and in this context explicates the Ten Commandments, thereby manifesting another Reformed tendency. The law is not only the threat that catalyzes the yearning for forgiveness through our recognition of our failures and restrains sin through fear of punishment, as it was for Luther, but it is also a useful and welcomed guide to direct the lives of the saints. (To be accurate, the Lutheran Melanchthon and even Luther himself did also uphold this "third use" of God's law, but the Reformed theologians ascribed much more significance to it.) We are saved in order to serve, and God's law is our friend and ally in that service. With confidence in God's grace, the Christian life unfolds as an expression of gratitude. God's redemptive grace is by no means cheap; it involves much more than the offer of forgiveness. This typical emphasis of the service that issues from heartfelt gratitude sustained the Reformed tradition's passionate concern for the disciplined life and for transformative action in the world.

On one other crucial matter, the understanding of the Eucharist, the catechism has usually been regarded as much more Reformed than Lutheran. At the Marburg Colloquy in 1529, Luther and Ulrich Zwingli, the reformer of Zurich in Switzerland, had attempted to come to a common understanding of all theological points, but sadly discovered that they could simply not agree on the interpretation of the Lord's Supper. Luther insisted upon a real physical presence of Jesus Christ, in, with, and under the elements of the bread and wine, while Zwingli maintained that the ritual stimulates us to remember the life, death, and resurrection of Jesus, with the elements functioning as symbols. To further complicate matters, John Calvin of Geneva later taught that believers are really united by the Holy Spirit to Christ who is spiritually present through the celebration of the Eucharist (a position that Luther's colleague Melanchthon approximated). When we "lift up our hearts to the Lord," we spiritually commune with the vital energy of the risen Christ in heaven. In this controversy the sentiments expressed in the Heidelberg Catechism may tend more toward Calvin's view, although a Zwinglian interpretation is not clearly ruled out.

On most issues the catechism succeeded in identifying existential motifs upon which moderate Lutherans, Calvinists, and even Zwinglians could agree. Its authors generally avoided the temptation to try to clarify Christian convictions by locating them in some metaphysical conceptual system borrowed from Plato, Aristotle, the late medieval theologians, or any other source. Instead, they illumined the meaning of Christian doctrines by illustrating the crucial roles that they play in living the Christian life. For example, God's sovereignty was not treated as a speculative problem concerning the exact mode of the operation of God's agency in relation to creaturely actions and events, but as a practical matter concerning the reassurance of troubled and frightened human beings. By resisting the impulse to situate doctrines in some theoretic framework, Ursinus, Olevianus, and their team avoided divisive scholastic disputes and foregrounded the unifying practice of piety. In the pages of the catechism, doctrines come to have significance and meaning as they are used to nurture Christainly appropriate hopes, sorrows, joys, and longings. This focus on the passions of the Christian life may account for the catechism's extraordinary and enduring influence.

Notes on the Translation

This translation is based on the first three editions of the catechism in German from 1563, as well as on the Latin version of 1563. I have favored the German version, except in instances where the meaning is clearer in the Latin text. I have sought throughout to express the content of the catechism in the natural rhythms of the English language, which sometimes involved breaking complex German sentences down into shorter English ones. I am deeply indebted to the Tercentenary edition of 1863 with its parallel columns of German text, Latin text, and English translation, which had been prepared by Emmanuel Gerhart, John Nevin, Henry Harbaugh, and others. I am also grateful for the work of Allen Miller, M. Eugene Osterhaven, Aladar Komjathy, and James McCord, who produced the masterful and eloquent four hundredth anniversary translation of the catechism. Like them, I have included the biblical references cited by the catechism's authors, quoted in the New Revised Standard Version translation, as well as the division of the catechism's questions into a series of fifty-two units appropriate for fifty-two Sundays. My labors would not have been possible without their admirable efforts.

THE HEIDELBERG CATECHISM

1. OUR ONLY COMFORT

LORD'S DAY 1

Question 1

What is your only comfort in life and in death?

That I belong, both body and soul and in life and in death,[a] not to myself,[b] but to my faithful savior Jesus Christ,[c] who has totally paid for all my sins[d] with his precious blood[e] and completely liberated me from the power of the devil,[f] and who takes care of me so well[g] that not a hair can fall from my head without the will of my Father in heaven.[h] In fact, everything must work together for my salvation.[i] Besides this, by his Holy Spirit he also assures me of eternal life[j] and makes me wholeheartedly willing and ready to live for him from now on.[k]

a. ROM. 14:8. If we live, we live to the Lord, and if we die, we die to the Lord; so then, whether we live or whether we die, we are the Lord's.

b. 1 COR. 6:19–20. Or do you not know that your body is a temple of the Holy Spirit within you, which you have from God, and that you are not your own? For you were bought with a price; therefore glorify God in your body.

c. 1 COR. 3.23. . . . and you belong to Christ, and Christ belongs to God.

d. JOHN 1:7; 2:2 . . . but if we walk in the light as he himself is in the light, we have fellowship with one another, and the blood of Jesus his Son cleanses us from all sin . . . and he is the atoning sacrifice for our sins, and not for ours only but also for the sins of the whole world.

e. 1 PET. 1:18–19. You know that you were ransomed from the futile ways inherited from your ancestors, not with perishable things like silver or gold, but with the precious blood of Christ, like that of a lamb without defect or blemish.

f. 1 JOHN 3:8. Everyone who commits sin is a child of the devil; for the devil has been sinning from the beginning. The Son of God was revealed for this purpose, to destroy the works of the devil.

Cf. HEB. 2:14.

g. JOHN 6:35, 39. Jesus said to them, "I am the bread of life. Whoever comes to me will never be hungry, and whoever believes in me will never be thirsty. And this is the will of him who sent me, that I should lose nothing of all that he has given me, but raise it up on the last day."

h. MATT. 10:29–31. "Are not two sparrows sold for a penny? Yet not one of them will fall to the ground apart from your Father. And even the hairs of your head are all counted. So do not be afraid; you are of more value than many sparrows."

Cf. Luke 21:16–18.

i. Rom 8:28. We know that all things work together for good for those who love God, who are called according to his purpose.

j. 2 Cor. 1:21–22. But it is God who establishes us with you in Christ and has anointed us, by putting his seal on us and giving us his Spirit in our hearts as a first installment.

Cf. 2 Cor. 5:5; Rom. 8:16; Eph. 1:14.

k. Rom. 8:14, 17. For all who are led by the Spirit of God are children of God...and if children, then heirs, heirs of God and joint heirs with Christ—if, in fact, we suffer with him so that we may also be glorified with him.

Question 2
How many things must you know that you may live and die in this blissful comfort?

Three things:[a] First, the magnitude of my sin and wretchedness.[b] Second, how I am released from all my sins and misery.[c] Third, how I am to be grateful to God for such redemption.[d]

a. Titus 3:3–8. For we ourselves were once foolish, disobedient, led astray, slaves to various passions and pleasures, passing our days in malice and envy, despicable, hating one another. But when the goodness and loving kindness of God our Savior appeared, he saved us, not because of any works of righteousness that we had done, but according to his mercy, through the water of rebirth and the renewal by the Holy Spirit. This Spirit he poured out on us richly through Jesus Christ our Savior, so that, having been justified by his grace, we might become heirs according to the hope of eternal life. The saying is sure.

b. JOHN 9:41. Jesus said to them, "If you were blind you would not have sin. But now that you say 'we see,' your sin remains."

Cf. ROM. 1:18–3:20.

c. JOHN 17:1–3. After Jesus had spoken these words, he looked up to heaven and said, "Father, the hour has come; glorify your Son so that the Son may glorify you, since you have given him authority over all people, to give eternal life to all whom you have given him. And this is eternal life, that they may know you, the only true God, and Jesus Christ whom you have sent."

Cf. ROM. 3:21–8:39; PHIL. 2:5–11; ACTS 10:34–43.

d. I PET. 2:9–10. But you are a chosen race, a royal priesthood, a holy nation, God's own people, in order that you may proclaim the mighty acts of him who called you out of darkness into his marvelous light. Once you were not a people, but now you are God's people; once you had not received mercy, but now you have received mercy.

Cf. ROM. 12–14; EPH. 5:8–10.

Part I. Humanity's Sin and Guilt—The Law of God

2. OUR HUMAN GUILT

LORD'S DAY 2

Question 3
How do you learn of your misery?

From the law of God.[a]

a. ROM. 3:20. For "no human being will be justified in [God's} sight" by deeds prescribed by the law, for through the law comes the knowledge of sin.

Cf. ROM. 7:7–25.

Question 4
What does the law of God require of us?

Christ teaches us this in a summary in Matthew 22:37–40: "'You shall love the Lord your God with all your heart, and with all your soul, and with all your mind.'[a] This is the greatest and first commandment. And a second is like it: 'You shall love your neighbor as yourself.'[b] On these two commandments hang all the law and the prophets." (Cf. Luke 10:27.)

a. Cf. Deut. 6:5.

b. Cf. Lev. 19:18.

Question 5

Can you do all this perfectly?

No,[a] for I am by nature prone to hate God and my neighbor.[b]

a. ROM. 3:10, 23. There is no one who is righteous, not even one . . . since all have sinned and fall short of the glory of God.

1 JOHN 1:8. If we say that we have no sin, we deceive ourselves and the truth is not in us.

b. ROM. 8:7–8. For this reason the mind that is set on the flesh is hostile to God; it does not submit to God's law — indeed it cannot, and those who are in the flesh cannot please God.

Cf. EPH. 2:1–3; TITUS 3:3.

LORD'S DAY 3

Question 6

Did God create human being evil and damaged?

No,[a] on the contrary, God created human being good and in God's own image,[b] that is, in genuine righteousness and holiness,[c] so that we might truly know God our creator, love God wholeheartedly, and live with God in eternal blessedness, in order to praise and glorify God.[d]

a. GEN. 1:31. God saw everything that he had made, and indeed, it was very good.

b. GEN. 1:27. So God created humankind in his image, in the image of God he created him; male and female he created them.

c. Eph. 4:24. . . . . clothe yourself with the new self, created according to the likeness of God in true righteousness and holiness.

d. Rev. 21:3. And I heard a loud voice from the throne saying, "See, the home of God is among mortals. He will dwell with them as their God; they will be his peoples, and God himself will be with them. . . ."

Question 7
From where, then, does this corrupt nature of human beings come?

From the fall and disobedience of our first parents, Adam and Eve, in the Garden of Eden.[a] Through this our nature became so corrupted[b] that we are all conceived and born in sin.[c]

a. Gen. 3:1–6. Now the serpent was more crafty than any other wild animal that the Lord God had made. He said to the woman, "Did God say, 'You shall not eat from any tree in the garden?'" The woman said to the serpent, "We may eat of the fruit of the trees in the garden; but God said, 'You shall not eat of the fruit of the tree that is in the middle of the garden, nor shall you touch it, or you shall die.'" But the serpent said to the woman, "You shall not die; for God knows that when you eat of it your eyes will be opened, and you will be like God, knowing good and evil." So when the woman saw that the tree was good for food, and that it was a delight to the eyes, and that the tree was to be desired to make one wise, she took of its fruit and ate; and she also gave some to her husband, who was with her, and he ate.

b. Rom. 5:12. Therefore, just as sin came into the world through one man, and death came through sin, and so death spread to all because all have sinned. . . .

c. Ps. 51.5. Indeed, I was born guilty, a sinner when my mother conceived me.

Question 8

But are we so corrupt that we are totally unable to do any good and are prone to do all evil?

Yes,[a] unless we are born again through God's Spirit.[b]

a. GEN. 6:5. The Lord saw that the wickedness of humankind was great in the earth, and that every inclination of the thoughts of their hearts was only evil continually.

ISA. 53.6. All we like sheep have gone astray; we have all turned to our own way.

JOB 14:4. Who can bring a clean thing out of an unclean? No one can.

JOHN 3:6. Jesus answered . . . "What is born of the flesh is flesh, and what is born of the Spirit is spirit."

b. JOHN 3:5. Jesus answered, "Very truly, I tell you, no one can enter the kingdom of God without being born of water and Spirit."

LORD'S DAY 4

Question 9

Does not God treat humanity unjustly, by requiring people in God's law to do something that they cannot do?

No, for God so created humanity that they could do it;[a] but humans, through the instigation of the devil,[b] have robbed themselves and all their descendants of this ability.[c]

a. GEN. 1:31. God saw everything that he had made, and indeed, it was very good.

b. JOHN 8:44. Jesus said to them ". . . You are of your father the devil, and you chose to do your father's desires. He was a murderer from the beginning and does not stand in the truth, because there was no truth in him. When he lies, he speaks according to his own nature, for he is a liar and the father of lies."

c. ROM. 5:12, 18–19. Therefore, just as sin came into the world through one man, and death came through sin, and so death spread to all because all have sinned. . . . Therefore just as one man's trespass led to condemnation for all, so one man's act of righteousness leads to justification and life for all. For just as by the one man's disobedience the many were made sinners, so by the one man's obedience the many will be made righteous.

Cf. Gen. 3.

3. THE JUDGMENT AND GRACE OF GOD

Question 10
Will God allow such disobedience and rebellion to go unpunished?

Certainly not, for God is terribly angry with our inborn sinfulness as well as our actual sins,[a] and will punish them according to God's righteous judgment in time and in eternity. As God has declared, "Cursed is everyone who does not observe and obey all the things written in the law."[b]

a. ROM. 1:18. For the wrath of God is revealed from heaven against all ungodliness and wickedness of those who by their wickedness suppress the truth.

b. GAL. 3:10. For all who rely on the works of the law are under a curse; for it is written, "Cursed is everyone who does not observe and obey all the things written in the book of the law."

Cf. Deut. 27:26; 28:15.

Question 11
But is not God also merciful?

God is indeed merciful,[a] but God is also righteous.[b] Consequently, God's righteousness requires that sin committed against the most high majesty of God must be punished with extreme, that is, with eternal punishment of both body and soul.[c]

a. EXOD. 34:6–7. The Lord passed before him and proclaimed, "The Lord, the Lord, a God merciful and gracious, slow to anger, and abounding in steadfast love and faithfulness, keeping steadfast love for the thousandth generation, forgiving iniquity and transgression and sin . . ."

b. EXOD. 20:5. ". . . for I the Lord your God am a jealous God, punishing children for the iniquity of parents, to the third and fourth generation of those who reject me . . ."

Ps. 5:4–6. For you are not a God who delights in wickedness; evil will not sojourn with you. The boastful will not stand before your eyes; you hate all evildoers. You destroy those who speak lies; the Lord abhors the bloodthirsty and deceitful.

c. MATT. 25:45–46. "Then [the King] will answer them, 'Truly I tell you, just as you did not do it to one of the least of these, you did not do it to me.' And these will go away into eternal punishment, but the righteous into eternal life."

Part II. Humanity's Redemption and Freedom—The Grace of God in Jesus Christ

4. JUSTIFICATION BY GRACE

LORD'S DAY 5

Question 12
Since, then, according to the righteous judgment of God we have deserved temporal and eternal punishment, how may we escape this punishment and be reconciled to God, being received with favor?

God wills that the divine justice must be satisfied;[a] therefore full payment must be made to God's justice, either by ourselves or by someone else.[b]

a. EXOD. 23:7. [God said,] ". . . I will not acquit the guilty." Cf. EXOD. 20:5; 34:7; DEUT. 7:9–11.

b. ROM. 8:3–4. For God has done what the law, weakened by the flesh, could not do: by sending his own Son in the likeness of sinful flesh, and to deal with sin, he condemned sin in the flesh, so that the just requirement of the law might be fulfilled in us, who walk not according to the flesh but to the Spirit.

Question 13
Can we make this payment ourselves?

By no means; rather, we daily make our guilt greater.[a]

a. JOB 9:3. If one wished to contend with [God], one could not answer him once in a thousand.

ROM. 2:4–5. Do you not realize that God's kindness is meant to lead you to repentance? But by your hard and impenitent heart you are storing up wrath for yourself on the day of wrath, when God's righteous judgment will be revealed.

MATT. 6:12. "And forgive us our debts, as we also have forgiven our debtors."

Question 14
But can any mere creature make the payment for us?

None. First of all, God will not punish any other creature for humanity's guilt.[a] Furthermore, no mere creature can bear the burden of God's eternal wrath against sin and deliver others from it.[b]

a. EZEK. 18:20. The person who sins shall die.

HEB. 2:14–15. Since, therefore, the children share flesh and blood, [Jesus] himself likewise shared the same things, so that through death he might destroy the one who has the power of death, that is, the devil, and free those who all their lives were held in slavery by the fear of death.

b. PS. 130:3. If you, O Lord, should mark iniquities, Lord, who could stand?

Question 15
What sort of mediator and redeemer must we seek then?

One who is a true[a] and righteous human being,[b] and yet stronger than all creatures; in other words, one who is simultaneously true God.[c]

a. 1 COR. 15:21. For since death came through a human being, the resurrection of the dead has also come through a human being. . . .

b. ISA. 53:9. They made his grave with the wicked and his tomb with the rich, although he had done no violence, and there was no deceit in his mouth.

HEB. 7:26. For it was fitting that we should have such a high priest, holy, blameless, undefiled, separated from sinners, and exalted above the heavens.

2 COR. 5:12. For our sake [God] made him to be sin who knew no sin, so that in him we might become the righteousness of God.

c. ISA. 9:6. For a child has been born for us, a son given to us; authority rests upon his shoulders; and he is named Wonderful Counselor, Mighty God, Everlasting Father, Prince of Peace.

Cf. Jer. 23:5–6.

LORD'S DAY 6

Question 16
Why must he be a true and righteous human being?

Because the justice of God requires[a] that the same human nature which has sinned should pay for sin, but anyone who is a sinner cannot make payment for others.[b]

a. Rom. 5:12, 15. Therefore, just as sin came into the world through one man, and death came through sin, and so death spread to all because all have sinned. . . . But the free gift is not like the trespass. For if the many died through the one man's trespass, much more surely have the grace of God and the free gift in the grace of the one man, Jesus Christ, abounded for the many.

b. 1 Pet. 3:18. For Christ also suffered for sins once for all, the righteous for the unrighteous, in order to bring you to God. He was put to death in the flesh, but made alive in the spirit . . .

Cf. Isa. 53:3–5, 10–11.

Question 17
Why must he simultaneously be true God?

So that by the power of his divinity he might bear in his humanity the burden of God's wrath;[a] and so regain righteousness and life for us[b] and restore them to us.[c]

a. Isa. 53:8. By a perversion of justice (the Lord's Servant) was taken away. Who could have imagined his future? For he was cut off from the land of the living, stricken for the transgressions of my people.

b. Acts 2:23–24. . . . this (Jesus), handed over to you according to the definite plan and foreknowledge of God, you crucified and killed by the hands of those outside the law. But God raised him up, having freed him from death, because it was impossible for him to be held in its power.

JOHN 1:4. . . . in him was life, and the life was the light of all people.

c. JOHN 3:16. For God so loved the world that he gave his only Son, so that everyone who believes in him may not perish but have life eternal.

2 COR. 5:21. For our sake (God) made him to be sin who knew no sin, so that in him we might become the righteousness of God.

Question 18
But who is this mediator who is simultaneously true God and a true and righteous human being?

Our Lord Jesus Christ[a] who is freely given to us for total redemption and righteousness.[b]

a. MATT. 1:23. Look, the virgin will conceive and bear a son, and they shall name him Emmanuel, which means "God with us."

LUKE 2:11. . . . to you is born this day in the city of David a Savior, who is the Messiah, the Lord.

Cf. 1 TIM. 3:16.

b. 1 COR. 1:30. He is the source of your life in Jesus Christ, who became for us wisdom from God, and righteousness and sanctification and redemption . . .

5. THE HOLY TRINITY

Question 19
From where do you know this?

From the holy gospel, which God's own self revealed in the beginning in the Garden of Eden,[a] then proclaimed through the holy patriarchs[b] and prophets,[c] and foreshadowed through the sacrifices and other ceremonies of the law,[d] and finally fulfilled through God's own well-beloved Son.[e]

a. GEN. 3:14–15. The Lord God said to the serpent, ". . . I will put enmity between you and the woman, and between your offspring and hers; he will strike your head, and you will strike his heel."

b. GEN. 22:18. "…and by your offspring shall all the nations of the earth gain blessing for themselves, because you obeyed my voice."

GEN. 49:10. The scepter shall not depart from Judah, nor the ruler's staff from between his feet, until tribute comes to him, and the obedience of the peoples is his.

c. HEB. 1:1–2. Long ago God spoke to our ancestors in many and various ways by the prophets, but in these last days he has spoken to us by a Son, whom he appointed heir to all things, through whom he also created the worlds.

ACTS 10:43. All the prophets testify about him [Jesus] that everyone who believes in him receives forgiveness of sins through his name.

Cf. Rom. 1:1–6; ACTS 3:22–26.

d. HEB. 9:13–15. For if the blood of goats and bulls, with the sprinkling of the ashes of a heifer, sanctifies those who have been defiled so that their flesh is purified, how much more will the blood of Christ, who through the eternal Spirit offered himself without blemish to God, purify our conscience from dead works to worship the living God! For this reason he is the mediator of a new covenant . . .

Cf. Heb. 9:1–10:10.

e. Gal. 4:4–5. But when the fullness of time had come, God sent his Son, born of a woman, born under the law, in order to redeem those who were under the law, so that we might receive adoption as children.

Cf. Rom. 10:4.

Lord's Day 7

Question 20
Will all people, then, be saved through Christ, just as they became lost through Adam?

No. Only those who are grafted into him by true faith and accept all his benefits.[a]

a. John 1:11–13. He came to what was his own, and his own people did not accept him. But to all who received him, who believed in his name, he gave power to become children of God, who were born, not of blood or of the will of the flesh or of the will of man, but of God.

Rom. 11:17–20. But if some of the branches were broken off, and you, a wild olive shoot, were grafted in their place to share the rich root of the olive tree, do not boast over the branches. If you do boast, remember that it is not you that support the root, but the root that supports you. You will say, "Branches were broken off so that I might be grafted in." That is true. They were broken off because of their unbelief, but you stand only through faith. So do not become proud, but stand in awe.

Heb. 4:2; 10:39. For indeed the good news came to us just as to them; but the message they heard did not benefit them, because they were not united by faith with those who listened. . . . But we were not among those who shrink back and so are lost, but among those who have faith and so are saved.

Cf. Isa. 53:11; Heb. 11.

Question 21

What is true faith?

It is not only a sure knowledge by which I affirm as true everything that God has revealed to us in God's Word,[a] but also a wholehearted trust that the Holy Spirit brings about in me[b] through the Gospel.[c] It is an assurance that not only to others but also to me God has freely given the forgiveness of sins, eternal righteousness, and salvation, by grace alone solely for the sake of Christ's worth.[d]

a. John 17:3. "And this is eternal life, that they may know you, the only true God, and Jesus Christ whom you have sent."

Cf. James 1:18.

b. Rom. 4:13, 16. For the promise that he would inherit the world did not come to Abraham or to his descendants through the law but through the righteousness of faith. . . . For this reason it depends on faith, in order that the promise may rest on grace and be guaranteed to all his descendants, not only to the adherents of the law but also to those who share the faith of Abraham (for he is the father of all of us . . .).

Matt. 16:15–17. He said to them, "But who do you say that I am?" Simon Peter answered, "You are the Messiah, the Son of the living God." And Jesus answered him,

"Blessed are you, Simon son of Jonah! For flesh and blood has not revealed this to you, but my Father in heaven."

2 COR. 1:21–22. But it is God who establishes us with you in Christ and has anointed us, by putting his seal on us and giving us his Spirit in our hearts as a first installment.

c. ROM. 1:16. For I am not ashamed of the gospel; it is the power of God for salvation to everyone who has faith, to the Jew first and also to the Greek.

ROM. 10:17. So faith comes from what is heard, and what is heard comes through the word of Christ.

d. ROM. 3:21–26. But now, apart from the law, the righteousness of God has been disclosed, and is attested by the law and the prophets, the righteousness of God through faith in Jesus Christ for all who believe. For there is no distinction, since all have sinned and fall short of the glory of God; they are now justified by his grace as a gift, through the redemption that is in Christ Jesus, whom God put forward as a sacrifice of atonement by his blood, effective through faith. He did this to show his righteousness, because in his divine forbearance he had passed over the sins previously committed; it was to prove at the present time that he himself is righteous and that he justifies the one who has faith in Jesus.

Cf. EPH. 2:4–9; GAL. 2:15–16.

Question 22
What, then, is it necessary for a Christian to believe?

Everything that is promised to us in the Gospel,[a] which is taught to us in summary form in the articles of the Apostles' Creed, our universal and undoubted confession of faith.

a. JOHN 20:31. But these are written so that you may come to believe that Jesus is the Messiah, the Son of God, and that through believing you may have life in his name.

Cf. MATT. 28:18–20; ACTS 10:34–43.

Question 23
What are these articles?

I believe in God the Father Almighty, Maker of heaven and earth, and in Jesus Christ, his only-begotten Son our Lord: who was conceived by the Holy Spirit, born of the Virgin Mary; suffered under Pontius Pilate, was crucified, dead, and buried; he descended into hell, the third day he rose again from the dead; he ascended into heaven and sits at the right hand of God the Father Almighty; from thence he shall come to judge the living and the dead.

I believe in the Holy Spirit; the holy catholic church; the communion of saints; the forgiveness of sins; the resurrection of the body; and the life everlasting.

LORD'S DAY 8

Question 24
How are these articles organized?

Into three parts: The first deals with God the Father and our creation, the second with God the Son and our redemption, and the third with God the Holy Spirit and our sanctification.

Question 25
Since there is only one divine being,[a] why do you speak of three: Father, Son, and Holy Spirit?

Because God has revealed God's own self in God's Word in such a way that these three distinct persons are the one, true, eternal God.[b]

a. DEUT. 6:4. Hear, O Israel: The Lord is our God, the Lord alone.

b. MATT. 3:16–17. And when Jesus had been baptized, just as he came up from the water, suddenly the heavens were opened to him and he saw the Spirit of God descending like a dove and alighting on him. And a voice from heaven said, "This is my Son, the Beloved, with whom I am well pleased."

Cf. MATT. 28:19; 2 COR. 13:14.

6. GOD THE FATHER

LORD'S DAY 9

Question 26
What do you believe when you say, "I believe in God the Father Almighty, Maker of heaven and earth?"

That the eternal Father of our Lord Jesus Christ, who made heaven and earth with everything in them out of nothing,[a] and who also sustains and governs them by divine eternal council and providence,[b] is for the sake of Christ his Son also my God and my Father.[c] I so completely trust in God that I have no doubt that God will provide me with everything necessary for body and soul.[d] Furthermore, whatever evil God sends to me in this troubled life God will transform to my good,[e] for God is able to do it, being almighty, and God is also willing to do it, being a faithful father.[f]

a. Ps. 90:1–2. A Prayer of Moses, the man of God. Lord, you have been our dwelling-place in all generations. Before the mountains were brought forth, or ever you had formed the earth and the world, from everlasting to everlasting you are God.

   Isa. 44:24. Thus says the Lord, your Redeemer, who formed you in the womb: "I am the Lord, who made all things, who alone stretched out the heavens, who by myself spread out the earth."

   Cf. Gen. 1; John 1:1–5; Ps. 33:6.

b. Matt. 10:29. "Are not two sparrows sold for a penny? Yet not one of them will fall to the ground unperceived by your Father."

   Cf. Ps. 104; Heb. 1:1–3.

c. Rom. 8:15–16. For you did not receive a spirit of slavery to fall back into fear, but you have received a spirit of adoption. When we cry, "Abba! Father!" it is that very Spirit bearing witness with our spirit that we are children of God. . . .

   Cf. John 1:12–13; Gal. 4:4–7.

d. Luke 12:22. He said to his disciples, "Therefore I tell you, do not worry about your life, what you will eat, or about your body, what you will wear."

   Cf. Matt. 6:25–44.

e. Rom. 8:28. We know that all things work together for good for those who love God, who are called according to his purpose.

f. Matt. 7:9–11. "Is there anyone among you who, if your child asks for bread, will give a stone? Or if the child asks for a fish, will give a snake? If you then, who are evil, know how to give good gifts to your children, how much more will your Father in heaven give good things to those who ask him!"

LORD'S DAY 10

Question 27
What do you understand by the providence of God?

The almighty and everywhere present power of God,[a] through which God still sustains heaven and earth, together with all creatures,[b] as if by God's own hand. God's power so governs them that plants and grass, rain and drought, fruitful and barren years, food and drink,[c] health and sickness,[d] riches and poverty,[e] and all things, come to us not by chance but by God's fatherly hand.[f]

a. ACTS 17:24–25. The God who made the world and everything in it, he who is Lord of heaven and earth, does not live in shrines made by human hands, nor is he served by human hands, as though he needed anything, since he himself gives to all mortals life and breath and all things.

Cf. ACTS 17:26–28.

b. HEB. 1:3. He is the reflection of God's glory and the exact imprint of God's very being, and he sustains all things by his powerful word. When he had made purification for sins, he sat down at the right hand of the Majesty on high. . . .

c. ACTS 14:15–17. Friends, why are you doing this? We are mortals just like you, and we bring you good news, that you should turn from these worthless things to the living God, who made the heaven and the earth and the sea and all that is in them. In past generations he allowed all the

nations to follow their own ways; yet he has not left himself without a witness in doing good—giving you rains
from heaven and fruitful seasons, and filling you with
food and your hearts with joy.

Cf. JER. 5:24.

d. John 9:3. Jesus answered, "Neither this man nor his parents sinned; he was born blind so that God's works might
be revealed in him."

e. PROV. 22:2. The rich and the poor have this in common:
the Lord is the maker of them all.

Cf. MATT. 10:29–31.

f. EPH. 1:11. In Christ we have also obtained an inheri-
tance, having been destined according to the purpose of
him who accomplishes all things according to his counsel
and will.

Question 28
*What do we gain by acknowledging that God has created
and still sustains all things?*

That we may be grateful in adversity,[a] thankful in prosper-
ity,[b] and trust our faithful God and Father for the future, certain that no creature will separate us from God's love,[c] since
all creatures are so thoroughly in God's hand that they cannot
even move without God's will.[d]

a. ROM. 5:3–4. And not only that, but we also boast in our
sufferings, knowing that suffering produces endurance,
and endurance produces character, and character produces hope. . . .

Cf. JAMES 1:3; JOB 1:21.

b. Deut. 8:10. You shall eat your fill and bless the Lord your God for the good land that he has given you.

c. Rom. 8:38–39. For I am convinced that neither death, nor life, nor angels, nor rulers, nor things present, nor things to come, nor powers, nor height, nor depth, nor anything else in all creation, will be able to separate us from the love of God in Christ Jesus our Lord.

d. Acts 17:28. For "In him we live and move and have our being"; as even some of your own poets have said, "For we too are his offspring."

Cf. Acts 17:25; Job 1:12; Prov. 21:1.

7. GOD THE SON

Lord's Day 11

Question 29
Why is the Son of God called Jesus, which means "Savior"?

Because he saves us from our sins,[a] and because salvation is not to be sought or found in anyone else.[b]

a. Matt. 1:21. "She will bear a son, and you are to name him Jesus, for he will save his people from their sins."

Cf. Heb. 7:25.

b. Acts 4:12. There is salvation in no one else, for there is no other name under heaven given among mortals by which we must be saved.

Question 30
Do those who seek their salvation and welfare through saints, their own selves, or anything else really believe in the only savior Jesus?

No. Even though they may boast of belonging to him, they deny the only savior Jesus by such actions.[a] For either Jesus is not a complete savior, or else those who by true faith receive this savior must possess in him everything that is necessary for their salvation.[b]

a. 1 COR. 1:12–13. What I mean is that each of you says, "I belong to Paul," or "I belong to Apollos," or "I belong to Cephas," or "I belong to Christ." Has Christ been divided? Was Paul crucified for you? Or were you baptized in the name of Paul?

   Cf. GAL. 5:4.

b. COL. 1:19–20. For in him all the fullness of God was pleased to dwell, and through him God was pleased to reconcile to himself all things, whether on earth or in heaven, by making peace through the blood of his cross.

   Cf. ISA. 9:6–7; JOHN 1:16.

LORD'S DAY 12

Question 31
Why is he called Christ, that is, the Anointed One?

Because he is ordained by God the Father and anointed by the Holy Spirit[a] to be our ultimate prophet and teacher,[b] who fully reveals to us God's secret council and will concerning our redemption,[c] and also to be our sole high priest,[d] who has redeemed us by the one sacrifice of his body and ever intercedes for us with the Father,[e] and also to be our eternal king, who governs us by his word and spirit, and defends and sustains us in the redemption he has gained for us.[f]

a. LUKE 3:21–22. Now when all the people were baptized, and when Jesus also had been baptized and was praying, the heaven was opened, and the Holy Spirit descended upon him in bodily form like a dove. And a voice came from heaven, "You are my Son, the Beloved; with you I am well pleased."

Cf. LUKE 4:14–19 (ISA. 61:1–2); HEB. 1:9.

b. ACTS 3:22. Moses said, "The Lord your God will raise up for you from your own people a prophet like me. You must listen to whatever he tells you."

Cf. DEUT. 18:15, 18.

c. JOHN 1:18. No one has ever seen God. It is God the only Son, who is close to the Father's heart, who has made him known.

Cf. JOHN 15:15.

d. HEB. 7:17. For it is attested of him, "You are a priest forever, according to the order of Melchizedek."

e. HEB. 9:12, 28. . . . he entered once for all into the Holy Place, not with the blood of goats and calves, but with his own blood, thus obtaining eternal redemption . . . so Christ, having been offered once to bear the sins of many, will appear a second time, not to deal with sin, but to save those who are eagerly waiting for him.

ROM. 8:34. Who is to condemn? It is Christ Jesus, who died, yes, who was raised, who is at the right hand of God, who indeed intercedes for us.

f. LUKE 1:32–33. He will be great, and will be called the Son of the Most High, and the Lord God will give to him the throne of his ancestor David. He will reign over the house of Jacob forever, and of his kingdom there will be no end.

ZECH. 9:9. Rejoice greatly, O daughter Zion! Shout aloud, O daughter Jerusalem! Lo, your king comes to you; triumphant and victorious is he, humble and riding on a donkey, on a colt, the foal of a donkey.

Cf. MARK 11:1–10; MATT. 21:1–11.

MATT. 28:18. And Jesus came and said to them, "All authority in heaven and on earth has been given to me."

Question 32
But why are you called a Christian?

Because through faith I am a member of Christ[a] and therefore share in his anointing,[b] so that I can also confess his name,[c] offer myself as a living sacrifice of thankfulness to him,[d] and fight against sin and the devil throughout this life with a free and good conscience,[e] and hereafter reign with him in eternity over all creatures.[f]

a. ACTS 11:26. . . . and it was in Antioch that the disciples were first called "Christians."

b. ACTS 2:17. . . . "In the last days it will be, God declares, that I will pour out my Spirit upon all flesh, and your sons and your daughters shall prophesy, and your young men shall see visions, and your old men shall dream dreams."

   Cf. JOEL 2:28; 1 JOHN 2:27.

c. MATT. 10:5; 32. These twelve Jesus sent out with the following instructions. . . . "Everyone therefore who acknowledges me before others, I also will acknowledge before my Father in heaven. . . ."

d. ROM. 12:1. I appeal to you therefore, brothers and sisters, by the mercies of God, to present your bodies as a living sacrifice, holy and acceptable to God, which is your spiritual worship.

1 PET. 2:5, 9. . . . like living stones, let yourself be built into a spiritual house, to be a holy priesthood, to offer spiritual sacrifices acceptable to God through Jesus Christ. . . . But you are a chosen race, a royal priesthood, a holy nation, God's own people in order that you may proclaim the mighty acts of him who called you out of darkness into his marvelous light.

e. 1 TIM. 1:18–19. I am giving you these instructions, Timothy, my child, in accordance with the prophecies made earlier about you, so that by following them you may fight the good fight, having faith and a good conscience.

f. 2 TIM. 2:11–13. The saying is sure: If we have died with him, we will also live with him; if we endure, we will also reign with him; if we deny him, he also will deny us; if we are faithless, he remains faithful—for he cannot deny himself.

LORD'S DAY 13

Question 33

Why is he called God's only-begotten Son, since we too are God's children?

Because only Christ is the natural, eternal Son of God,[a] while we are adopted as God's children for his sake by grace.[b]

a. JOHN 1:1–3, 14, 18. In the beginning was the Word, and the Word was with God, and the Word was God. He was in the beginning with God. All things came into being through him, and without him not one thing came into being. . . . And the Word became flesh and lived among us, and we have seen his glory, the glory as of a father's only son, full of grace and truth. . . . No one has ever seen God. It is God the only Son, who is close to the Father's heart, who has made him known.

Cf. HEB. 1:2.

b. EPH. 1:5–6. He destined us for adoption as his children through Jesus Christ, according to the good pleasure of his will, to the praise of his glorious grace that he freely bestowed on us in the Beloved.

Cf. JOHN 1:12; ROM. 8:15–17.

Question 34
Why do you call him our Lord?

Because, not with gold or silver but with his precious blood,[a] he has redeemed and purchased us body and soul from sin and the power of the devil to be his own.[b]

a. 1 PET. 1:18–19. You know that you were ransomed from the futile ways inherited from your ancestors, not with perishable things like silver and gold, but with the precious blood of Christ, like that of a lamb without defect or blemish.

Cf. 1 PET. 2:9–10.

b. 1 COR. 7:23. You were bought with a price; do not become slaves of human masters.

Cf. 1 COR. 6:20.

Lord's Day 14

Question 35

What is the meaning of "Conceived by the Holy Spirit, born of the Virgin Mary"?

That the eternal Son of God, who is and continues to be true and eternal God,[a] took upon himself our true human nature from the flesh and blood of the Virgin Mary[b] through the action of the Holy Spirit,[c] so that he could be the genuine seed of David,[d] like his fellow human beings in all things,[e] except for sin.[f]

a. JOHN 1:1. In the beginning was the Word, and the Word was with God, and the Word was God.

b. JOHN 1:14. And the Word became flesh and lived among us, and we have seen his glory, the glory as of a father's only son, full of grace and truth.

Cf. GAL. 4:4.

c. LUKE 1:35. The angel said to her, "The Holy Spirit will come upon you, and the power of the Most High will overshadow you; therefore the child to be born will be holy; he will be called the Son of God."

Cf. MATT. 1:18, 20.

d. ROM. 1:1–3. . . . the gospel of God (is) . . . the gospel concerning his Son, who was descended from David according to the flesh. . . .

Cf. PS. 132:11; 2 SAM. 7:12–17.

e. PHIL. 2:5–7. Let the same mind be in you that was in Jesus Christ, who, though he was in the form of God, did not regard equality with God as something to be exploited, but emptied himself, taking the form of a slave, being born in human likeness.

f. HEB. 4:15. For we do not have a high priest who is unable to sympathize with our weakness, but we have one who in every respect has been tested as we are, yet without sin.

Question 36
What good does the holy conception and birth of Christ do us?

That he is our mediator,[a] and that in God's sight he covers the sinfulness in which I was conceived with his innocence and perfect holiness.[b]

a. 1 TIM. 2:5–6. For there is one God; there is also one mediator between God and humankind, Christ Jesus, himself human, who gave himself a ransom for all—this was attested at the right time.

b. ROM. 4:7. Blessed are those whose iniquities are forgiven, and whose sins are covered. . . .

Cf. Ps. 32:1; 1 COR. 1:30.

LORD'S DAY 15

Question 37
What do you understand by the word "suffered"?

That during his entire life on earth, but especially at the end of it, he bore in body and soul the wrath of God against the whole human race,[a] so that through his suffering, as the only atoning sacrifice, he could redeem our body and soul from eternal damnation, and could gain for us God's grace, righteousness, and eternal life.[b]

a. Isa. 53:12. . . . . he poured out himself to death, and was numbered with the transgressors; yet he bore the sins of many, and made intercession for the transgressors.

1 Pet. 2:24. He himself bore our sins in his body on the cross, so that, free from sins, we might live for righteousness; by his wounds you have been healed.

b. Rom. 3:24–25. . . . they are now justified by his grace as a gift, through the redemption that is in Christ Jesus, whom God put forward as a sacrifice of atonement by his blood, effective through faith. He did this to show his righteousness, because in his divine forbearance he had passed over the sins previously committed. . . .

Cf. 1 John 2:2.

Question 38
Why did he suffer under the judge Pontius Pilate?

That he, being innocent, might be condemned by an earthly judge,[a] and through this deliver us from the severe judgment of God that should have fallen upon us.[b]

a. John 19:13–16. When Pilate heard these words, he brought Jesus outside and sat on the judge's bench at a place called The Stone Pavement, or in Hebrew Gabbatha. Now it was the day of the Preparation for the Passover; and it was about noon. He said to the Jews, "Here is your King!" They cried out, "Away with him! Away with Him! Crucify him!" Pilate asked them, "Shall I crucify your King?" The chief priests answered, "We have no king but the emperor." Then he handed him over to them to be crucified.

Cf. LUKE 23:13–24; ACTS 4:27–28.

b. ISA. 53:4–5. Surely he has born our infirmities and carried our diseases; yet we accounted him stricken, struck down by God and afflicted. But he was wounded for our transgressions, crushed for our iniquities; upon him was the punishment that made us whole, and by his bruises we are healed.

ROM. 5:6. For while we were still weak, at the right time Christ died for the ungodly.

Cf. 2 COR. 5:21; GAL. 3:13.

Question 39
Is there any more significance to the fact that he was crucified than there would be if he had died some other death?

Yes, for by this I am assured that he took upon himself the curse that lay upon me, because the death of the cross was cursed by God.[a]

a. GAL. 3:13. Christ redeemed us from the curse of the law by becoming a curse for us—for it is written, "Cursed is everyone who hangs on a tree" . . .

Cf. DEUT. 21–23.

LORD'S DAY 16

Question 40
Why did Christ have to suffer death?

Because the righteousness and truth of God require that nothing but the death of the Son of God could make satisfaction for our sins.[a]

a. HEB. 2:9. . . . but we do see Jesus, who for a little while
   was made lower than the angels, now crowned with glory
   and honor because of the suffering of death, so that by
   the grace of God he might taste death for everyone.

   Cf. ROM. 8:3–4.

Question 41

Why was he buried?

To make it clear that he was really dead.[a]

a. ACTS 13:29. When they had carried out everything that
   was written about him, they took him down from the tree
   and laid him in a tomb.

   Cf. MATT. 27:59–60; LUKE 23:50–55; JOHN 19:38–42.

Question 42

Then, since Christ died for us, why do we also have to die?

Our death is not a satisfaction for our sins,[a] but only a
dying to sin and an entering into eternal life.[b]

a. ROM. 7:24. Wretched man that I am! Who will rescue me
   from this body of death?

   Ps. 49:7. Truly, no ransom avails for one's life; there is
   no price one can give to God for it.

b. 1 THESS. 5:9–10. For God has destined us not for wrath
   but for obtaining salvation through our Lord Jesus Christ,
   who died for us, so that whether we are awake or asleep
   we may live with him.

   Cf. JOHN 5:24.

Question 43
What else do we gain from the sacrifice and death of Christ on the cross?

That by his power our old self is crucified, put to death, and buried with him,[a] so that the evil lusts of the flesh may reign in us no longer,[b] but that we may offer ourselves to him as a sacrifice of thanksgiving.[c]

a. ROM. 6:6. We know that our old self was crucified with him so that the body of sin might be destroyed, and we might no longer be enslaved to sin.
   Cf. COL. 2:12.

b. ROM. 6:12. Therefore, do not let sin exercise dominion in your mortal bodies, to make you obey their passions.

c. ROM. 12:1. I appeal to you therefore, brothers and sisters, by the mercies of God, to present your bodies as a living sacrifice, holy and acceptable to God, which is your spiritual worship.

Question 44
Why is "He descended into hell" added?

That in my most painful and gravest tribulations I may be assured that Christ my Lord has delivered me from hellish anguish and torment by the inexpressible anguish, pains, and terrors which he suffered in his soul both on the cross and earlier.[a]

a. ISA. 53:5. But he was wounded for our transgressions, crushed for our iniquities; upon him was the punishment that made us whole, and by his bruises we are healed.

MATT. 27:46. And about three o'clock Jesus cried with a loud voice, "Eli, Eli, lema sabachthani?" that is, "My God. My God, why have you forsaken me?"

LORD'S DAY 17

Question 45
What benefits do we gain from the resurrection of Christ?

First, by his resurrection he has overcome death so that he could make us share in the righteousness which he has gained for us through his death.[a] Second, by his power we too are raised up to a new life.[b] Third, the resurrection of Christ is a sure pledge to us of our blessed resurrection.[c]

a. ROM. 4:24–25. It will be reckoned to us who believe in him who raised Jesus our Lord from the dead, who was handed over to death for our trespasses and was raised for our justification.

Cf. HEB. 2:14–15; 1 PET. 1:3, 21.

b. ROM. 6:3–4. Do you not know that all of us who have been baptized into Christ Jesus were baptized into his death? Therefore we have been buried with him by baptism into death, so that, just as Christ was raised from the dead by the glory of the Father, so we too might walk in newness of life.

Cf. COL. 3:1–15; EPH. 2:4–6.

c. ROM. 8:11. If the Spirit of him who raised Jesus from the dead dwells in you, he who raised Christ from the dead will give life to your mortal bodies also through his Spirit that dwells in you.

Cf. 1 COR. 15.

Question 46

How do you understand the words "He ascended into heaven"?

That Christ was taken up from the earth into heaven before the eyes of the disciples[a] and continues there on our behalf[b] until he will come again to judge the living and the dead.[c]

a. LUKE 24:50–51. Then [Jesus] led them out as far as Bethany, and, lifting up his hands, he blessed them. While he was blessing them, he withdrew from them and was carried up into heaven.

   Cf. ACTS 1:9.a

b. HEB. 9:24. For Christ did not enter a sanctuary made by human hands, a mere copy of the true one, but he entered into heaven itself, now to appear in the presence of God on our behalf.

   Cf. ROM. 8:34; EPH. 4:8.

c. ACTS 1:11. They said, "Men of Galilee, why do you stand looking up toward heaven? This Jesus, who has been taken up from you into heaven, will come in the same way as you saw him go into heaven."

   ACTS 10:42. He commanded us to preach to the people and to testify that he is the one ordained by God as judge of the living and the dead.

   Cf. MATT. 25:31–46.

Question 47

Then, is Christ not with us until the end of the world, as he has promised us?

Christ is true human being and true God. In regard to his human nature he is no longer on earth,[b] but in regard to his divinity, majesty, grace, and Spirit, he is never absent from us.[c]

a. MATT. 28:20. "And remember, I am with you always, to the end of the age."

b. JOHN 17:11. "And now I am no longer in the world, but they are in the world, and I am coming to you. Holy Father, protect them in your name that you have given me, so that they may be one, as we are one."

Cf. JOHN 16:28.

c. JOHN 14:18–19. "I will not leave you orphaned; I am coming to you. In a little while the world will no longer see me; because I live, you also will live."

Question 48

But, in this way, are not the two natures in Christ separated from one another, if the humanity is not present wherever the divinity is?

By no means; for since the divinity is incomprehensible and present everywhere,[a] it must follow that the divinity is indeed beyond the bounds of the humanity which it has taken on. Nevertheless, the divinity is in that humanity as well, and remains personally united to it.[b]

a. JER. 23:23–24. Am I a God near by, says the Lord, and not a God far off? Who can hide in secret places so that I cannot see them? says the Lord. Do I not fill heaven and earth? says the Lord.

Cf. Ps. 139:7–10.

b. JOHN 3:13. "No one has ascended into heaven except the one who descended from heaven, the Son of Man."

COL. 2:9. For in [Christ] the whole fullness of deity dwells bodily. . . .

Question 49

What benefits do we gain from Christ's ascension into heaven?

First, that he is our advocate in the presence of his Father in heaven.[a] Second, that we have our flesh in heaven as a sure pledge that he, as the head, will also take us, his members, up to himself.[b] Third, that he will send us his Spirit, as a further pledge,[c] by whose power we seek those things that are above, where Christ sits at the right hand of God, and not the things that are on earth.[e]

a. ROM. 8:34. It is Christ Jesus, who died, yes, who was raised, who is at the right hand of God, who indeed intercedes for us.

Cf. 1 JOHN 2:1.

b. JOHN 14:2. "In my Father's house there are many dwelling places. If it were not so, would I have told you that I go to prepare a place for you?"

Cf. John 17:24; 20:17.

c. JOHN 14:16–17. "And I will ask the Father, and he will give you another Advocate, to be with you forever. This is the Spirit of truth, whom the world cannot receive, because it neither sees him nor knows him. You know him, because he abides with you, and he will be in you."

Cf. ACTS 2; 2 COR. 1:22; 5:5.

d. COL. 3:1. So if you have been raised with Christ, seek the things that are above, where Christ is, seated at the right hand of God.

Cf. PHIL. 3:20.

LORD'S DAY 19

Question 50
Why is "And sits at the right hand of God" added?

Because Christ ascended into heaven so that he might appear there as the head of his church,[a] through whom the Father governs all things.[b]

a. EPH. 1:20–23. God put this power to work in Christ when he raised him from the dead and seated him at his right hand in the heavenly places, far above all rule and authority and power and dominion, and above every name that is named, not only in this age but also in the age to come. And he has put all things under his feet and has made him the head over all things for the church, which is his body, the fullness of him who fills all in all.

Cf. COL. 1:18.

b. MATT. 28:18. And Jesus came and said to them, "All authority in heaven and on earth has been given to me."

Cf. JOHN 5:22.

Question 51
What do we benefit from this glory of Christ our head?

First, that by his Holy Spirit he showers heavenly gifts upon us, his members.[a] Then, that by his power he defends and preserves us against all enemies.[b]

a. ACTS 2:33. Being therefore exalted at the right hand of God, and having received from the Father the promise of the Holy Spirit, he has poured out this that you both see and hear.

EPH. 4:8. Therefore it is said, "When he ascended on high he made captivity itself a captive; he gave gifts to his people."

b. JOHN 10:28. "I gave them eternal life, and they will never perish. No one will snatch them out of my hand."

Question 52
How are you comforted by the "return of Christ to judge the living and the dead"?

That in all troubles and persecution I, with head held high, may look for the self-same one who has already offered himself to the judgment of God for me and has removed all the curse from me[a] to come again as judge from heaven; that he will cast all his enemies and mine into eternal condemnation,[b] but will take me, together with all his chosen ones, to himself into heavenly joy and glory.[c]

a. LUKE 21:28. "Now when these things begin to take place, stand up and raise your heads, because your redemption is drawing near."

PHIL. 3:20. But our citizenship is in heaven, and it is from there that we are expecting a savior, the Lord Jesus Christ.

b. MATT. 25:41–43. "Then he will say to those at his left hand, 'You that are accursed, depart from me into the eternal fire prepared for the devil and his angels; for I was hungry and you gave me no food, I was thirsty and you gave me nothing to drink, I was a stranger and you did not welcome me, naked and you did not give me clothing, sick and in prison and you did not visit me.'"

c. MATT. 25:34. "Then the king will say to those at his right hand, 'Come, you that are blessed by my Father, inherit the kingdom prepared for you from the foundation of the world. . . .'"

8. GOD THE HOLY SPIRIT

LORD'S DAY 20

Question 53
What do you believe about the Holy Spirit?

First, that the Spirit is eternal God equally with the Father and the Son.[a] Furthermore, that the Spirit is also given to me,[b] making me participate in Christ and all his benefits[c] through a true faith, comforting me, and abiding with me forever.[e]

a. GEN. 1:1–2. In the beginning when God created the heavens and the earth, the earth was a formless void and darkness covered the face of the deep, while a wind from God swept over the face of the waters.

JOHN 4:24. "God is spirit, and those who worship him must worship him in spirit and truth."

Cf. John 14:7–17; Acts 5:3–4.

b. MATT. 28:19. "Go therefore and make disciples of all nations, baptizing them in the name of the Father and of the Son and of the Holy Spirit. . . ."

1 COR. 3:16. Do you not know that you are God's temple and that God's Spirit dwells in you?

Cf. 2 Cor. 1:22.

c. 1 Cor. 6:17, 19. But anyone united to the Lord becomes one spirit with him. . . . Or do you not know that your body is a temple of the Holy Sprit within you, which you have from God, and that you are not your own?

Cf. Gal. 4:6–7.

d. Acts 89:31. Meanwhile the church throughout Judea, Galilee, and Samaria had peace and was built up. Living in fear of the Lord and in the comfort of the Holy Spirit, it increased in numbers.

e. John 14:16. "And I will ask the Father, and he will give you another Advocate, to be with you forever."

Lord's Day 21

Question 54
What do you believe about the holy catholic church?

That, out of the whole human race, from the beginning to the end of the world,[a] the Son of God,[b] by his Spirit and Word,[c] gathers, protects, and preserves for himself, in the unity of the true faith,[d] a chosen community for eternal life. I believe that I am and forever shall remain a living member of it.[e]

a. Gen 26:3b–4. ". . . I will fulfill the oath that I swore to your father Abraham. I will make your offspring as numerous as the stars of heaven, and will give to your offspring all these lands; and all the nations of the earth shall gain blessing for themselves through your offspring. . . ."

Rev. 5:9. They sing a new song: "You are worthy to take

the scroll and to open its seals, for you were slaughtered and by your blood you ransomed for God saints from every tribe and language and people and nation."

b. COL. 1:18. [Christ] is the head of the body, the church; he is the beginning, the firstborn from the dead, so that he might come to have first place in everything.

c. ISA. 59:21. And as for me, this is my covenant with them, says the Lord: my spirit that is upon you, and my words that I have put in your mouth, shall not depart out of your mouth, or out of the mouths of your children, or out of the mouths of your children's children, says the Lord, from now on and forever.

Cf. ROM. 1:16–18; 10:14–17.

d. ACTS 13:47–48. For so the Lord has commanded us, saying, "I have set you to be a light to the Gentiles, so that you may bring salvation to the ends of the earth." When the Gentiles heard this, they were glad and praised the word of the Lord, and as many as had been destined for eternal life became believers.

Cf. ISA. 49:6.

EPH. 4:3-6–3-6. . . . [make] every effort to maintain the unity of the Spirit in the bond of peace. There is one body and one Spirit, just as you were called to the one hope of your calling, one Lord, one faith, one baptism, one God and Father of all, who is above all and through all and in all.

EPH. 5:25–27. Husbands love your wives, just as Christ loved the church and gave himself up for her, in order to make her holy by cleansing her with the washing of water by the word, so as to present the church to himself in splendor, without a spot or wrinkle or anything of the kind—yes, so that she may be holy and without blemish.

e. JOHN 10:28. "I give them eternal life, and they will never perish. No one will snatch them out of my hand."

Cf. ROM. 8:29–39.

Question 55
What do you understand by "the communion of saints"?

First, that believers, each and every one, as members of Christ, share in one fellowship with Christ and all his treasures and gifts.[a] Second, that each one should feel obliged to use these gifts willingly and with joy for the benefit and welfare of other members.[b]

a. 1 COR. 1:9. God is faithful; by him you were called into the fellowship of his Son, Jesus Christ our Lord.

1 COR. 12:4–7, 12–13. Now there are a variety of gifts, but the same Spirit; and there are varieties of services, but the same Lord; and there are varieties of activities, but the same God who activates all of them in everyone. To each is given the manifestation of the Spirit for the common good. . . . For just as the body is one and has many members, and all the members of the body, though many, are one body, so it is with Christ. For in the one Spirit we were all baptized into one body—Jews or Greeks, slaves or free—and we were all made to drink of one Spirit.

b. 1 COR. 12:14, 21, 26–27. Indeed, the body does not consist of one member but of many. . . . The eye cannot say to the hand, "I have no need of you," nor again the head to the feet, "I have no need of you." . . . If one member suffers, all suffer together with it; if one member is honored, all rejoice together with it. Now you are the body of Christ and individually members of it.

1 COR. 13:4–5. Love is patient; love is kind; love is not envious or boastful or arrogant or rude. It does not insist on its own way; it is not irritable or resentful. . . .

Cf. PHIL. 2:1–11; 1 COR. 12–13.

Question 56
What do you believe about the forgiveness of sins?

That God, for the sake of Christ's reconciling work,[a] will no longer remember my sins or the sinful nature with which I must struggle for my entire life.[b] God graciously gives me the righteousness of Christ so that I may never be judged again.[c]

a. 2 COR. 5:19, 21. . . . in Christ God was reconciling the world to himself, not counting their trespasses against them, and entrusting the message of reconciliation to us . . . . For our sake he made him to be sin who knew no sin, so that in him we might become the righteousness of God.

Cf. 1 JOHN 1:7; 2:2.

b. JER. 31:34. No longer shall they teach one another, or say to each other, "Know the Lord," for they shall all know me, from the least of them to the greatest, says the Lord; for I will forgive their iniquity and remember their sin no more.

Cf. Ps. 103.

Rom. 8:1–2. There is therefore now no condemnation for those who are in Christ Jesus. For the law of the Spirit of life in Christ Jesus has set you free from the law of sin and of death.

c. John 3:17–18. "Indeed, God did not send the Son into the world to condemn the world, but in order that the world might be saved through him. Those who believe in him are not condemned. . . ."

Lord's Day 22

Question 57
What comfort does the resurrection of the body give you?

That after this life not only my soul shall be taken immediately up to Christ, its head,[a] but also that this body of mine, raised by the power of Christ, shall be united again with my soul, and will be made conformable to the glorious body of Christ.[b]

a. Luke 23:43. [Jesus] replied, "Truly I tell you, today you will be with me in Paradise."

Phil. 1:21. For to me, living is Christ and dying is gain.

b. I Cor. 15:20, 42–46, 54. But in fact Christ has been raised from the dead, the first fruits of those who have died. . . . So it is with the resurrection of the dead. What is sown is perishable, what is raised is imperishable. It is sown in dishonor, it is raised in glory. It is sown in weakness, it is raised in power. It is sown a physical body, it is raised a spiritual body. If there is a physical body, there is also a spiritual body. Thus it is written, "The first man, Adam, became a living being;" the last Adam became a life-giving spirit. But it is not the spiritual that is first, but the physical, and then the spiritual. . . . When this perishable body puts on imperishability, and this mortal body puts on immortality, then the saying that is written will be fulfilled: "Death is swallowed up in victory."

JOB 19:25. For I know that my Redeemer lives, and that at last he will stand upon the earth. . . .

1 JOHN 3:2. Beloved, we are God's children now; what we will be has not yet been revealed. What we do know is this: when he is revealed, we will be like him, for we will see him as he is.

PHIL. 3:21. [Jesus Christ] will transform the body of our humiliation that it may be conformed to the body of his glory, by the power that also enables him to make all things subject to himself.

Question 58
What comfort does the article about "the life everlasting" give you?

That, because I now feel in my heart the beginning of eternal joy,[a] I shall possess after this life perfect blessedness, which no eye has seen, nor ear heard, nor the human heart conceived,[b] and so praise God forever.[c]

a. ROM. 14:17. For the kingdom of God is not food and drink but righteousness and peace and joy in the Holy Spirit.

b. 1 COR. 2:9. But, as it is written, "What no eye has seen, nor ear heard, nor the human heart conceived, what God has prepared for those who love him"—these things God has revealed to us through the Spirit. . . .

c. JOHN 17:3. "And this is eternal life, that they may know you, the only true God, and Jesus Christ whom you have sent."

9. TRUE FAITH

LORD'S DAY 23

Question 59
But how are you helped now that you believe all this?

That I am righteous in Christ before God, and an heir of eternal life.[a]

a. ROM. 1:17. For in it the righteousness of God is revealed through faith for faith; as it is written, "The one who is righteous will live by faith."

Cf. HEB. 2:4.

ROM. 5:1. Therefore, since we are justified by faith, we have peace with God through our Lord Jesus Christ. . . .

JOHN 3:36. Whoever believes in the Son has eternal life; whoever disobeys the Son will not see life, but must endure God's wrath.

Question 60
How are you righteous before God?

Only by true faith in Jesus Christ.[a] Although my conscience accuses me that I have terribly sinned against all the commandments of God, and have not kept any of them,[b] and that I am still always prone to all evil,[c] nevertheless God, without any merit of my own,[d] out of sheer grace,[e] grants and imputes to me the perfect satisfaction, righteousness, and holiness of Christ.[f] It is as if I had never committed any sin or had ever had sinfulness in me,[g] and had myself performed all the obedience which Christ has carried out for me,[h] if only I accept such a blessing with a trusting heart.[i]

a. ROM. 3:21–22. But now, apart from law, the righteousness of God has been disclosed, and is attested by the law and the prophets, the righteousness of God through faith in Jesus Christ for all who believe.

   Cf. PHIL. 3:8–11.

b. ROM. 3:9–10. What then? Are we any better off? No, not at all; for we have already charged that all, both Jews and Greeks, are under the power of sin, as it is written: "There is no one who is righteous, not even one. . . ."

c. ROM. 7:23. . . . but I see in my members another law at war with the law of my mind, making me captive to the law of sin that dwells in my members.

d. TITUS 3:5. . . . he saved us, not because of any works of righteousness that we had done, but according to his mercy, through the water of rebirth and renewal by the Holy Spirit.

e. EPH. 2:8. For by grace you have been saved through faith, and this is not your own doing; it is the gift of God. . . .

   Cf. ROM. 3:24.

f. 1 JOHN 2:1–2. My little children, I am writing these things to you so that you may not sin. But if anyone does sin, we have an advocate with the Father, Jesus Christ the righteous; and he is the atoning sacrifice for our sins, and not for ours only but also for the sins of the whole world.

g. Rom. 4:24. It will be reckoned to us who believe in him who raised Jesus our Lord from the dead. . . .

Cf. 2 Cor. 5:21.

h. Rom. 4:3–5. For what does the scripture say? "Abraham believed God, and it was reckoned to him as righteousness." Now to one who works, wages are not reckoned as a gift but as something due. But to one who without works trusts him who justifies the ungodly, such faith is reckoned as righteousness.

i. Rom 3:24–25. . . . they are now justified by his grace as a gift, through the redemption that is in Christ Jesus, whom God put forward as a sacrifice of atonement by his blood, effective through faith. He did this to show his righteousness, because in his divine forbearance he had passed over the sins previously committed. . . .

Question 61
Why do you say that you are righteous by faith alone?

Not because I please God by the worthiness of my faith, but only because the satisfaction, righteousness, and holiness of Christ are my righteousness before God,[a] and because I can receive it and make it my own in no other way than by faith alone.

a. 1 Cor. 1:30; 2:2. He is the source of your life in Christ Jesus, who became for us wisdom from God, and righteousness and sanctification and redemption. . . . For I decided to know nothing among you except Jesus Christ, and him crucified.

LORD'S DAY 24

Question 62

But why cannot our good works be our righteousness before God, or at least a part of it?

Because the righteousness which can stand before the judgment of God must be utterly perfect and entirely in conformity with the divine law,[a] while even our best works in this life are all imperfect and tainted with sin.[b]

a. GAL. 3:10. For all who rely on the works of the law are under a curse; for it is written, "Cursed is everyone who does not observe and obey all the things written in the book of the law."

Cf. DEUT. 27:26.

b. ISA. 64:6. We have all become like one who is unclean, and all our righteous deeds are like a filthy cloth. We all fade like a leaf, and our iniquities, like the wind, take us away.

Question 63

But why do our good works earn nothing, even though it is God's will to reward them in this life and also in the future life?

This reward is not given because of worthiness, but out of grace.[a]

a. LUKE 17:10. "So you also, when you have done all that you were ordered to do, say, 'We are worthless slaves; we have done only what we ought to have done!'"

Question 64
But does not this doctrine make people careless and depraved?

No, because it is impossible for those who are grafted into Christ by true faith to fail to produce the fruit of thankfulness.[a]

a. MATT 7:16–17. You will know them by their fruits. Are grapes gathered from thorns, or figs from thistles? In the same way, every good tree bears good fruit, but the bad tree bears bad fruit.

   JOHN 15:5. I am the vine, you are the branches. Those who abide in me and I in them bear much fruit, because apart from me you can do nothing.

10. THE HOLY SACRAMENTS

LORD'S DAY 25

Question 65
Then, since faith alone makes us share in Christ and all his blessings, where does such faith come from?

The Holy Spirit awakens it in our hearts[a] by the preaching of the holy gospel,[b] and confirms it by the use of the holy sacraments.

a. EPH. 2:8. For by grace you have been saved through faith, and this is not your own doing; it is the gift of God. . . .

   Cf. JOHN 3:5.

b. 1 PET. 1:23, 25. You have been born anew, not of perishable but of imperishable seed, through the living and enduring word of God. . . . "but the word of the Lord endures forever." That word is the good news that was announced to you.

Cf. Matt. 28:19–20.

Question 66
What are the sacraments?

They are visible, holy signs and seals[a] instituted by God so that God may use them to more fully reveal and seal to us the promise of the gospel, namely, that God graciously grants us the forgiveness of sins and eternal life for the sake of the one sacrifice of Christ accomplished on the cross.[b]

a. Rom. 4:11. He received the sign of circumcision as a seal of the righteousness that he had by faith while he was still uncircumcised. The purpose was to make him the ancestor of all who believe without being circumcised and who thus have righteousness reckoned to them. . . .

   Cf. Gen. 17:11; Deut. 30:6.

b. Acts 2:38, 22:16. Peter said to them, "Repent, and be baptized every one of you in the name of Jesus Christ so that your sins may be forgiven; and you will receive the gift of the Holy Spirit. And now why do you delay? Get up, be baptized, and have your sins washed away, calling on his name."

   Cf. Heb. 9.

Question 67
Then, are both the word and the sacraments designed to direct our faith to the sacrifice of Jesus Christ on the cross as the only foundation of our salvation?

Yes, indeed, for the Holy Spirit teaches in the gospel and confirms by the holy sacraments that our whole salvation is based upon the one sacrifice of Christ offered on the cross for us.[a]

a. ROM. 6:3. Do you not know that all of us who have been baptized into Christ Jesus were baptized into his death?

GAL. 3:27. As many of you as were baptized into Christ have clothed yourselves with Christ.

1 COR. 11:26. For as often as you eat this bread and drink the cup, you proclaim the Lord's death until he comes.

Question 68
In the New Testament how many sacraments has Christ instituted?

Two: holy baptism and the holy supper.

11. HOLY BAPTISM

LORD'S DAY 26

Question 69
How does holy baptism confirm for you and assure you that you share in the one sacrifice of Christ on the cross?

In this way: Christ has instituted this outward washing with water[a] and has promised[b] by it that I am just as certainly washed with his blood and spirit from the corruption of my soul, that is, from all my sins, as I am washed outwardly with water that commonly washes away the filth from my body.[c]

a. MATT. 28:19. Go therefore and make disciples of all nations, baptizing them in the name of the Father and of the Son and of the Holy Spirit. . . .

Cf. ACTS 2:38.

b. MATT. 3:11. "I baptize you with water for repentance, but one who is more powerful than I is coming after me; I am not worthy to carry his sandals. He will baptize you with the Holy Spirit and fire."

Cf. ROM. 6:3–10. Do you not know that all of us who have been baptized into Christ Jesus were baptized into his death? Therefore we have been buried with him by baptism into death, so that, just as Christ was raised from the dead by the glory of the Father, so we too might walk in newness of life. For if we have been united with him in a death like his, we will certainly be united with him in a resurrection like his. We know that our old self was crucified with him so that the body of sin might be destroyed, and we might no longer be enslaved to sin. For whoever has died is freed from sin. But if we have died with Christ, we believe that we will also live with him. We know that Christ, being raised from the dead, will never die again; death no longer has dominion over him. The death he died, he died to sin, once for all; but the life he lives, he lives to God.

c. I PET. 3:21. And baptism, which this prefigured, now saves you—not as a removal of dirt from the body, but as an appeal to God for a good conscience, through the resurrection of Jesus Christ. . . .

Question 70

What does it mean to be washed with the blood and spirit of Christ?

It means to have the forgiveness of sins from God, through grace, for the sake of Christ's blood which he shed for us in his sacrifice on the cross,[a] and also to be renewed by the Holy Spirit and sanctified as members of Christ, so that we may more and more die to sin and lead holy and blameless lives.[b]

a. EPH. 1:7. In him we have redemption through his blood, the forgiveness of our trespasses, according to the riches of his grace.

Cf. HEB. 12:24; 1 PET. 1:2; REV. 1:5–6.

b. 1 COR. 6:11. And this is what some of you used to be. But you were washed, you were sanctified, you were justified in the name of the Lord Jesus Christ and in the Spirit of our God.

ROM. 6:4. Therefore we have been buried with him by baptism into death, so that, just as Christ was raised from the dead by the glory of the Father, so we too might walk in newness of life.

Cf. JOHN 1:33; COL. 2:12.

Question 71

Where has Christ promised that we are as certainly washed with his blood and Spirit as with the water of baptism?

In the institution of baptism, which says: "Go therefore and make disciples of all nations, baptizing them in the name of the Father, and of the Son, and of the Holy Spirit."[a] "Any one who believes and is baptized will be saved, but anyone who does not believe will be condemned."[b] This promise is also repeated where Scripture calls baptism "the bath of rebirth"[c] and "the washing away of sins."[d]

a. MATT. 28:19. "Go therefore and make disciples of all nations, baptizing them in the name of the Father and of the Son and of the Holy Spirit. . . ."

b. MARK 16:16. "The one who believes and is baptized will be saved; but the one who does not believe will be condemned."

c. TITUS 3:5. . . . he saved us, not because of any works of righteousness that we had done, but according to his mercy, through the water of rebirth and renewal by the Holy Spirit.

d. ACTS 22:16. "'And now why do you delay? Get up, be baptized, and have your sins washed away, calling on his name.'"

LORD'S DAY 27

Question 72
Then, is the outward washing with water itself the washing away of sins?

No,[a] for only the blood of Jesus Christ and the Holy Spirit cleanse us from all sin.[b]

a. MATT. 3:11. "I baptize you with water for repentance, but one who is more powerful than I is coming after me; I am not worthy to carry his sandals. He will baptize you with the Holy Spirit and fire."

EPH. 5:25B–26. Husbands, love your wives, just as Christ loved the church and gave himself up for her, in order to make her holy by cleansing her with the washing of water by the word. . . .

Cf. I PET. 3:21.

b. I JOHN 1:7. . . . but if we walk in the light as he himself is in the light, we have fellowship with one another, and the blood of Jesus his Son cleanses us from all sin.

I COR. 6:11. But you were washed, you were sanctified, you were justified in the name of the Lord Jesus Christ and in the Spirit of our God.

Question 73
Then why does the Holy Spirit call baptism the bath of rebirth and the washing away of sins?

God does not speak in this way without a powerful reason. Namely, through baptism God teaches us that just as the filthiness of the body is removed by water, so also are our sins taken away by the blood and Spirit of Christ.[a] But even more importantly, God seeks to assure us by the divine pledge and sign that we are just as truly washed from our sins spiritually as our bodies are washed with water.[b]

a. REV. 7:14. I said to him, "Sir, you are the one that knows." Then he said to me, "These are they who have come out of the great ordeal; they have washed their robes and made them white in the blood of the Lamb."

Cf. 1 Cor. 6:11.

b. GAL. 3:27. As many of you as were baptized into Christ have clothed yourselves with Christ.

Question 74
Should infants also be baptized?

Yes, because they, as well as their parents, belong to the covenant and the people of God.[a] Since both redemption from sin through the blood of Christ and the Holy Spirit who awakens faith are promised to them no less than to their parents,[b] children are also to be taken into the Christian church and distinguished from the children of unbelievers by baptism, as a sign of the covenant.[c] Something like this was done in the old covenant by circumcision,[d] which baptism has been instituted to replace.[e]

a. GEN. 17:7. I will establish my covenant between me and you, and your offspring after you throughout their generations, for an everlasting covenant, to be God to you and to your offspring after you.

MATT. 19:14. But Jesus said, "Let the little children come to me, and do not stop them; for it is to such as these that the kingdom of heaven belongs."

b. ACTS 2:38–39. Peter said to them, "Repent, and be baptized every one of you in the name of Jesus Christ so that your sins may be forgiven; and you will receive the gift of the Holy Spirit. For the promise is for you, for your children, and for all who are far away, everyone whom the Lord our God calls to him."

Cf. ISA. 44:1–3; LUKE 1–15.

c. ACTS 10:47. "Can anyone withhold the water for baptizing these people who have received the Holy Spirit just as we have?"

1 COR. 7:14. For the unbelieving husband is made holy through his wife, and the unbelieving wife is made holy

through her husband. Otherwise, your children would be unclean, but as it is, they are holy.

d. Cf. GEN. 17:9–14.

e. COL. 2:11–13. In him also you were circumcised with a spiritual circumcision, by putting off the body of the flesh in the circumcision of Christ; when you were buried with him in baptism, you were also raised with him through faith in the power of God, who raised him from the dead. And when you were dead in trespasses and the uncircumcision of your flesh, God made you alive together with him, when he forgave us all our trespasses. . . .

12. THE HOLY LORD'S SUPPER

LORD'S DAY 28

Question 75
How does the Holy Supper testify to you and assure you that you share in the one sacrifice of Christ on the cross and in all his benefits?

In this way: Christ has commanded me and all believers to eat of this broken bread and to drink of this cup in memory of him, and by doing so has promised:[a] first, that his body was offered and broken on the cross for me, and his blood was shed for me, as certainly as I see with my eyes the bread of the Lord broken for me and the cup shared with me. Moreover, he has also promised that he himself feeds and nourishes my soul to everlasting life with his crucified body and shed blood just as certainly as I receive from the hand of the minister and actually taste the bread and cup of the Lord which are given to me as true signs of the body and blood of Christ.

a. see Question 77 below.

Question 76

What does it mean to eat the crucified body and drink the shed blood of Christ?

It is not only to embrace with a trusting heart all the sufferings and death of Christ, and by so doing receive the forgiveness of sins and eternal life,[a] but also to be united more and more to his sacred body by the Holy Spirit who dwells both in Christ and in us,[b] so that, although he is in heaven[c] and we are on earth, we nevertheless are flesh of his flesh and bone of his bone,[d] and live and are governed forever by one Spirit, just as the members of our bodies are governed by one soul.[e]

a. JOHN 6:35, 40. Jesus said to them, "I am the bread of life. Whoever comes to me will never be hungry, and whoever believes in me will never be thirsty. . . . This is indeed the will of my Father, that all who see the Son and believe in him may have eternal life; and I will raise them up on the last day."

JOHN 6:53–54. So Jesus said to them, "Very truly, I tell you, unless you eat the flesh of the Son of Man and drink his blood, you have no life in you. Those who eat my flesh and drink my blood have eternal life, and I will raise them up on the last day. . . ."

b. JOHN 6:56. "Those who eat my flesh and drink my blood abide in me, and I in them."

c. ACTS 3:20–21. . . . so that times of refreshing may come from the presence of the Lord, and that he may send the Messiah appointed for you, that is, Jesus, who must remain in heaven until the time of universal restoration that God announced long ago through his holy prophets.

Cf. ACTS 1:9–11; 1 COR. 11:26.

d. EPH. 5:30. . . . because we are members of his body.

Cf. 1 Cor. 6:15, 17, 19.

e. 1 JOHN 3:24b. All who obey his commandments abide in him, and he abides in them. And by this we know that he abides in us, by the Spirit that he has given us.

EPH. 4:15–16. But speaking the truth in love, we must grow up in every way into him who is the head, into Christ, from whom the whole body, joined and knit together by every ligament with which it is equipped, as each part is working properly, promotes the body's growth in building itself up in love.

Cf. JOHN 6:56–58; 15:1–6.

Question 77

Where has Christ promised that he will feed and nourish believers with his body and blood just as certainly as they eat of this broken bread and drink of this cup?

In the institution of the Lord's Supper which states: The Lord Jesus on the night when he was betrayed took bread, and when he had given thanks, he broke it, and said, "This is my body which is for you. Do this in remembrance of me." In the same way also the cup, after supper, saying, "This cup is the new covenant in my blood. Do this, as often as you drink it, in remembrance of me." For as often as you eat this bread and drink this cup, you proclaim the Lord's death until he comes.[a]

This promise is repeated also by the apostle Paul: when we bless "the cup of blessing," is it not a means of sharing the body of Christ? Because there is one loaf, we, many as we are, are one body; for it is one loaf of which we all partake.[b]

a. I COR. 11:23–26. For I received from the Lord what I also handed on to you, that the Lord Jesus on the night when he was betrayed took a loaf of bread, and when he had given thanks, he broke it and said, "This is my body that is for you. Do this in remembrance of me." In the same way he took the cup also, after supper, saying, "This cup is the new covenant in my blood. Do this, as often as you drink it, in remembrance of me." For as often as you eat this bread and drink the cup, you proclaim the Lord's death until he comes.

Cf. MATT. 26:26–28; MARK 14:22–24; LUKE 22:19.

b. I COR. 10:16–17. The cup of blessing that we bless, is it not a sharing in the blood of Christ? The bread that we break, is it not a sharing in the body of Christ? Because there is one bread, we who are many are one body, for we all partake of the one bread.

LORD'S DAY 29

Question 78
Do the bread and the wine become the actual body and blood of Christ?

No, for as the water in baptism is not changed into the blood of Christ, nor becomes by itself the means of washing away sins, but is only a divine sign and assurance of it, so also in the Lord's Supper[a] the sacred bread does not become the body of Christ itself,[b] although agreeing with the nature and use of the sacraments,[c] it is called the body of Christ.

a. MATT. 26:26–29. While they were eating, Jesus took a loaf of bread, and after blessing it he broke it, gave it to the disciples, and said, "Take, eat; this is my body." Then he took a cup, and after giving thanks he gave it to them, saying, "Drink from it, all of you; for this is my blood of the covenant, which is poured out for many for the forgiveness of sins. I tell you, I will never again drink of this fruit of the vine until that day when I drink it new with you in my Father's kingdom."

b. I COR. 11:26–28. For as often as you eat this bread and drink the cup, you proclaim the Lord's death until he comes. Whoever, therefore, eats the bread or drinks the cup of the Lord in an unworthy manner will be answerable for the body and blood of the Lord. Examine yourselves, and only then eat of the bread and drink of the cup.

c. I COR. 10:1–4. I do not want you to be unaware, brothers and sisters, that our ancestors were all under the cloud, and all passed through the sea, and all were baptized into Moses in the cloud and in the sea, and all ate the same spiritual food, and all drank the same spiritual drink. For they drank from the spiritual rock that followed them, and the rock was Christ.

Cf. Gen. 17:10–19; EXOD. 12:27, 43, 48.

Question 79
Then why does Christ call the bread his body, and the cup his blood, or the new covenant in his blood, and why does St. Paul call it a means of sharing in the body and blood of Christ?

Christ does not speak like this without a good reason: namely, to teach us that as bread and wine sustain this temporal life so also his crucified body and shed blood are the true meat and drink of our souls for eternal life.[a] He also speaks like this to assure us by this visible sign and pledge that we share in his true body and blood through the working of the Holy Spirit just as certainly as we receive with our mouth these holy tokens in remembrance of him,[b] and that all his sufferings and obedience are as certainly our own as if we ourselves had suffered and satisfied God in our own persons.

a. JOHN 6:51, 55. "I am the living bread that came down from heaven. Whoever eats of this bread will live forever; and the bread that I will give for the life of the world is my flesh . . . for my flesh is true food and my blood is true drink."

b. 1 COR. 10:16–17. The cup of blessing that we bless, is it not a sharing in the blood of Christ? The bread that we break, is it not a sharing in the body of Christ? Because there is one bread, we who are many are one body, for we all partake of the one bread.

LORD'S DAY 30

Question 80
What is the difference between the Lord's Supper and the papal Mass?

The Lord's Supper testifies to us that we have complete forgiveness of all our sins through the one sacrifice of Jesus Christ which he himself has accomplished on the cross once and for all time[a] (and that through the Holy Spirit we are ingrafted into Christ,[b] who now is in heaven with his true body at the right hand of God the Father,[c] and is to be worshiped there).[d] But the Mass teaches that the living and the dead do not have forgiveness of sins through the sufferings of Christ unless Christ is offered again daily for them by the priests (and that Christ is present bodily under the form of bread and wine and is therefore to be worshiped in them). Consequently the Mass is basically nothing else than a denial of the once and for all sacrifice and passion of Jesus Christ[e] (and therefore is a condemnable idolatry).

Note: Parts of this question first appeared in the second 1563 edition of the catechism. The portions in parentheses were not added until the third edition of 1563.

a. HEB. 7:27; 9:12, 25–28. Unlike the other high priests, he has no need to offer sacrifices day after day, first for his own sins, and then for those of the people; this he did once for all when he offered himself. . . . he entered once for all into the Holy Place, not with the blood of goats and calves, but with his own blood, thus obtaining eternal redemption. . . . Nor was it to offer himself again and again, as the high priest enters the Holy Place year after year with blood that is not his own; for then he would have had to suffer again and again since the foundation of the world. But as it is, he has appeared once for all at the end of the age to remove sin by the sacrifice of himself. And just as it is appointed for mortals to die once, and after that the judgment, so Christ, having been offered once to bear the sins of many, will appear a second time, not to deal with sin, but to save those who are eagerly waiting for him.

Cf. HEB. 10:10–18.

b. 1 COR. 6:17. But anyone united to the Lord becomes one spirit with him.

c. HEB. 1:3; 8:1. He is the reflection of God's glory and the exact imprint of God's very being, and he sustains all things by his powerful word. When he had made purification for sins, he sat down at the right hand of the Majesty on high. . . . Now the main point in what we are saying is this: we have such a high priest, one who is seated at the right hand of the throne of the Majesty in the heavens. . . .

d. JOHN 20:17. Jesus said to her, "Do not hold on to me, because I have not yet ascended to the Father. But go to my brothers and say to them, 'I am ascending to my Father and your Father, to my God and your God.'"

ACTS 7:55–56. But filled with the Holy Spirit, he gazed into heaven and saw the glory of God and Jesus standing at the right hand of God. "Look," he said, "I see the heavens opened and the Son of Man standing at the right hand of God!"

COL. 3:1. So if you have been raised with Christ, seek the things that are above, where Christ is, seated at the right hand of God.

Cf. JOHN 4:21–24; PHIL. 3:20; 1 THESS. 1:10.

e. HEB. 9:25–26; 10:11–14. Nor was it to offer himself again and again, as the high priest enters the Holy Place year after year with blood that is not his own; for then he would have had to suffer again and again since the foundation of the world. But as it is, he has appeared once for all at the end of the age to remove sin by the sacrifice of himself. . . . And every priest stands day after day at his service, offering again and again the same sacrifices that can never take away sins. But when Christ had offered for all time a single sacrifice for sins, "he sat down at the right hand of God," and since then has been waiting "until his enemies would be made a footstool for his feet." For by a single offering he has perfected for all time those who are sanctified.

13. CHURCH DISCIPLINE

Question 81
Who should come to the table of the Lord?

Those who are dissatisfied with themselves for their sins,[a] and yet trust that these sins have been forgiven them and that their remaining weakness is covered by the passion and death of Christ,[b] and who also desire more and more to strengthen their faith and amend their life.[c] But the impenitent and the hypocrites eat and drink judgment to themselves.[d]

a. MATT. 5:3. "Blessed are the poor in spirit, for theirs is the kingdom of heaven."

b. Ps. 103:2–3. Bless the Lord, O my soul, and do not forget all his benefits — who forgives all your iniquity, who heals all your diseases.

   EPH. 1:7. In him we have redemption through his blood, the forgiveness of our trespasses, according to the riches of his grace.

c. MATT. 5:5. "Blessed are the meek, for they will inherit the earth."

d. 1 COR. 10:21; 11:28. You cannot drink the cup of the Lord and the cup of demons. You cannot partake of the table of the Lord and the table of demons. Examine yourselves, and only then eat of the bread and drink of the cup.

Question 82

Should those who reveal themselves to be unbelieving and godless by their testimony and life be admitted to this Supper?

No, for this would profane the covenant of God, and God's wrath would be provoked against the entire congregation.[a] Therefore the Christian church is obligated, according to the ordinance of Christ and his apostles, by the office of the keys, to exclude such people until they reform their lives.

a. 1 COR. 11:20, 26–29, 34. When you come together, it is not really to eat the Lord's supper. . . . For as often as you eat this bread and drink the cup, you proclaim the Lord's death until he comes. Whoever, therefore, eats the bread or drinks the cup of the Lord in an unworthy manner will be answerable for the body and blood of the Lord. Examine yourselves, and only then eat of the bread and drink of the cup. For all who eat and drink without discerning the body, eat and drink judgment against themselves. . . . If you are hungry, eat at home, so that when you come together, it will not be for your condemnation. About the other things I will give instructions when I come.

Cf. ISA. 1:11–15; 66:3; Ps. 50:16.

LORD'S DAY 31

Question 83

What is the office of the keys?

The preaching of the holy gospel and church discipline. By these two means the kingdom of heaven is opened to believers and shut against unbelievers.[a]

a. MATT. 16:19. "I will give you the keys of the kingdom of heaven, and whatever you bind on earth will be bound in heaven, and whatever you loose on earth will be loosed in heaven."

JOHN 20:23. "If you forgive the sins of any, they are forgiven them; if you retain the sins of any, they are retained."

Question 84
How is the kingdom of heaven opened and shut by the preaching of the holy gospel?

In this way: according to the command of Christ, the kingdom of heaven is opened to believers, one and all, when it is proclaimed and openly testified that as often as they accept the promise of the gospel with true faith all their sins are really forgiven them by God for the sake of Christ's worthiness. On the other hand, the wrath of God and eternal condemnation abide on all unbelievers and hypocrites as long as they do not repent.[a] According to the witness of this gospel, God will judge both in this life and in the life to come.

a. MATT. 28:19. "Go therefore and make disciples of all nations, baptizing them in the name of the Father and of the Son and of the Holy Spirit. . . ."

JOHN 20:21–23. Jesus said to them again, "Peace be with you. As the Father has sent me, so I send you." When he had said this, he breathed on them and said to them, "Receive the Holy Spirit. If you forgive the sins of any, they are forgiven them; if you retain the sins of any, they are retained."

MATT. 16:19. "I will give you the keys of the kingdom of heaven, and whatever you bind on earth will be bound in heaven, and whatever you loose on earth will be loosed in heaven."

Cf. JOHN 3:18–36; ROM. 2:2–17.

Question 85
How is the kingdom of heaven shut and opened by church discipline?

In this way: according to the command of Christ all those who call themselves "Christian" but espouse un-Christian doctrines or live in an un-Christian manner should be offered caring admonition. If they still refuse to turn from their error or evil ways, complaint about them should be brought to the church or to its proper officers. Then, if they neglect this warning, they are to be excluded from the holy sacraments and the communion of the church and by God from the realm of Christ.[a] But if they promise and show a real transformation, they should be received again as members of Christ and of the church.[b]

a. MATT. 18:15–18. "If another member of the church sins against you, go and point out the fault when the two of you are alone. If the member listens to you, you have regained that one. But if you are not listened to, take one or two others along with you, so that every word may be confirmed by the evidence of two or three witnesses. If the member refuses to listen to them, tell it to the church; and if the offender refuses to listen even to the church, let such a one be to you as a Gentile and a tax collector. Truly I tell you, whatever you bind on earth will be bound in heaven, and whatever you loose on earth will be loosed in heaven."

1 Cor. 5:11–13. But now I am writing to you not to associate with anyone who bears the name of brother or sister who is sexually immoral or greedy, or is an idolater, reviler, drunkard, or robber. Do not even eat with such a one. For what have I to do with judging those outside? Is it not those who are inside that you are to judge? God will judge those outside. "Drive out the wicked person from among you."

Cf. 2 Thess. 3:14; 2 John 10–11.

b. Luke 15:18. "I will get up and go to my father, and I will say to him, 'Father, I have sinned against heaven and before you. . . .'"

Cf. 2 Cor. 2:6–11.

Part III. Our Thankfulness and Obedience—New Life through the Holy Spirit

14. DISCIPLINE AND GOOD WORKS

LORD'S DAY 32

Question 86

Since we are redeemed from all sin and misery by grace through Christ, without deserving it, why must we do good works?

Because Christ, having redeemed us with his blood, also renews us in his own image through his Holy Spirit. Consequently, we may show with our whole lives how grateful we are to God for God's goodness[a] and we can glorify God through our lives.[b] Furthermore, we ourselves may be assured of our faith by its fruits[c] and we can win our neighbors to Christ by our godly conduct.[d]

a. ROM. 6:13; 12:1. No longer present your members to sin as instruments of wickedness, but present yourselves to God as those who have been brought from death to life, and present your members to God as instruments of righteousness. I appeal to you therefore, brothers and sisters, by the mercies of God, to present your bodies as a living sacrifice, holy and acceptable to God, which is your spiritual worship.

Cf. 1 PET. 2:5–10.

b. MATT. 5:16. "In the same way, let your light shine before others, so that they may see your good works and give glory to your Father in heaven."

1 COR. 6:19–20. Or do you not know that your body is a temple of the Holy Spirit within you, which you have from God, and that you are not your own? For you were bought with a price; therefore glorify God in your body.

Cf. 1 PET. 2:12.

c. MATT. 7:17. "In the same way, every good tree bears good fruit, but the bad tree bears bad fruit."

Cf. LUKE 13:6–9.

GAL. 5:22–24. By contrast, the fruit of the Spirit is love, joy, peace, patience, kindness, generosity, faithfulness, gentleness, and self-control. There is no law against such things. And those who belong to Christ Jesus have crucified the flesh with its passions and desires.

d. 1 PET. 3:1–2. Wives, in the same way, accept the authority of your husbands, so that, even if some of them do not obey the word, they may be won over without a word by their wives' conduct, when they see the purity and reverence of your lives.

Question 87
Can those who do not turn to God from their unthankful, unrepentant lives be saved?

Certainly not; for as Scripture says no fornicator, idolater, adulterer, thief, greedy person, drunkard, slanderer, robber, or anyone like that shall inherit the kingdom of God.[a]

a. 1 COR. 6:9–10. Do you not know that wrongdoers will not inherit the kingdom of God? Do not be deceived! Fornicators, idolaters, adulterers, male prostitutes, sodomites, thieves, the greedy, drunkards, revilers, robbers — none of these will inherit the kingdom of God.

Cf. GAL. 5:19–21; EPH. 5:5–33; 1 JOHN 3:14–24.

LORD'S DAY 33

Question 88

How many aspects does true repentance or conversion have?

Two: the dying of the old self and the birth of the new.[a]

a. ROM. 6:4–6. Therefore we have been buried with him by baptism into death, so that, just as Christ was raised from the dead by the glory of the Father, so we too might walk in newness of life. For if we have been united with him in a death like his, we will certainly be united with him in a resurrection like his. We know that our old self was crucified with him so that the body of sin might be destroyed, and we might no longer be enslaved to sin.

2 COR. 5:17. So if anyone is in Christ, there is a new creation: everything old has passed away; see, everything has become new!

Cf. Eph. 4:22–24; COL. 3:5–10; 1 COR. 5:7.

Question 89
What is the dying of the old self?

Sincere sorrow over our sins, increasing hatred of them, and flight from them.[a]

a. ROM. 8:13. . . . for if you live according to the flesh, you will die; but if by the Spirit you put to death the deeds of the body, you will live.

2 COR. 7:10. For godly grief produces a repentance that leads to salvation and brings no regret, but worldly grief produces death.

Cf. JOEL 2:13; PS. 51:3, 8, 17.

Question 90
What is the birth of the new self?

Sincere joy in God through Christ[a] and delight in living according to the will of God in all good works.[b]

a. ROM. 5:1. Therefore, since we are justified by faith, we have peace with God through our Lord Jesus Christ. . . .

Cf. ROM. 14:17; ISA. 57:15.

b. GAL. 2:20. . . . and it is no longer I who live, but it is Christ who lives in me. And the life I now live in the flesh I live by faith in the Son of God, who loved me and gave himself for me.

Cf. ROM. 6:10–11.

Question 91
But what are good works?

Only those that are motivated by true faith,[a] in accord with the Law of God,[b] and done for God's glory,[c] and not those that are based on our own opinion or on human traditions.[d]

a. ROM. 14:20B, 22B–23. Do not, for the sake of food, destroy the work of God. Everything is indeed clean, but it is wrong for you to make others fall by what you eat. . . . The faith that you have, have as your own conviction before God. Blessed are those who have no reason to condemn themselves because of what they approve. But those who have doubts are condemned if they eat, because they do not act from faith; for whatever does not proceed from faith is sin.

b. 1 SAM. 15:22. And Samuel said, "Has the Lord as great delight in burnt offerings and sacrifices, as in obeying the voice of the Lord? Surely, to obey is better than sacrifice, and to heed than the fat of rams."

Cf. EPH. 2:10.

c. 1 COR. 10:31. So, whether you eat or drink, or whatever you do, do everything for the glory of God.

d. DEUT. 12:32. You must diligently observe everything that I command you; do not add to it or take anything from it.

MATT. 15:9. ". . . in vain do they worship me, teaching human precepts as doctrines."

Cf. ISA. 29:13; EZEK. 20:18–19.

LORD'S DAY 34

Question 92
What is the Law of God?

GOD SPOKE ALL THESE WORDS, SAYING:

FIRST COMMANDMENT

"I am the Lord your God, who brought you out of the land of Egypt, out of the house of slavery; you shall have no other gods before me."

SECOND COMMANDMENT

"You shall not make for yourself an idol, whether in the form of anything that is in heaven above, or that is in the earth beneath, or that is in the water under the earth. You shall not bow down to them or worship them; for I the Lord your God am a jealous God, punishing children for the iniquity of parents, to the third and fourth generation of those who reject me, but showing steadfast love to the thousandth generation of those who love me and keep my commandments."

THIRD COMMANDMENT

"You shall not make wrongful use of the name of the Lord your God, for the Lord will not acquit anyone who misuses his name."

FOURTH COMMANDMENT

"Remember the Sabbath day, and keep it holy. Six days you shall labor, and do all your work. But the seventh day is a sabbath to the Lord your God; you shall not do any work–you, your son or your daughter, your male or female slave, your livestock, or the alien resident in your towns. For in six days the Lord made heaven and earth, the sea, and all that is in them, but rested the seventh day; therefore the Lord blessed the sabbath day and consecrated it."

FIFTH COMMANDMENT

"Honor your father and your mother, so that your days may be long in the land that the Lord your God is giving you."

SIXTH COMMANDMENT

"You shall not murder."

SEVENTH COMMANDMENT

"You shall not commit adultery."

EIGHTH COMMANDMENT

"You shall not steal."

NINTH COMMANDMENT

"You shall not bear false witness against your neighbor."

TENTH COMMANDMENT

"You shall not covet your neighbor's house; you shall not covet your neighbor's wife, or male or female slave, or ox, or donkey, or anything that belongs to your neighbor."[a]

a. EXOD. 20:1–17. Then God spoke all these words: I am the Lord your God, who brought you out of the land of Egypt, out of the house of slavery; you shall have no other gods before me. You shall not make for yourself an idol, whether in the form of anything that is in heaven above, or that is on the earth beneath, or that is in the water under the earth. You shall not bow down to them or worship them; for I the Lord your God am a jealous God, punishing children for the iniquity of parents, to the third and the fourth generation of those who reject me, but showing steadfast love to the thousandth generation of those who love me and keep my commandments. You shall not make wrongful use of the name of the Lord your God, for the Lord will not acquit anyone who misuses his name. Remember the sabbath day, and keep it holy. Six days you shall labor and do all your work. But the seventh day is a sabbath to the Lord your God; you shall not do any work—you, your son or your daughter, your male or female slave, your livestock, or the alien resident in your towns. For in six days the Lord made heaven and earth, the sea, and all that is in them, but rested the seventh day; therefore the Lord blessed the sabbath day and consecrated it. Honor your father and your mother, so that your days may be long in the land that the Lord your God is giving you. You shall not murder. You shall not commit adultery. You shall not steal. You shall not bear false witness against your neighbor. You shall not covet your neighbor's house; you shall not covet your neighbor's wife, or male or female slave, or ox, or donkey, or anything that belongs to your neighbor.

Cf. Deut. 5:6–21.

Question 93
How are these commandments divided?

Into two tables:[a] the first one teaches us in four commandments what our duties to God are; the second one teaches us in six commandments what our duties to our neighbor are.[b]

a. EXOD. 34:28–29. He was there with the Lord forty days and forty nights; he neither ate bread nor drank water. And he wrote on the tablets the words of the covenant, the ten commandments. Moses came down from Mount Sinai. As he came down from the mountain with the two tablets of the covenant in his hand, Moses did not know that the skin of his face shone because he had been talking with God.

Cf. Deut. 4:13; 10:3.

b. Matt. 22:37–39. He said to him, "'You shall love the Lord your God with all your heart, and with all your soul, and with all your mind.' This is the greatest and first commandment. And a second is like it: 'You shall love your neighbor as yourself.'"

15. LOVE AND HONOR TO GOD — THE FIRST TABLE OF THE LAW

Question 94
What does God require in the first commandment?

That I must avoid and flee all idolatry,[a] sorcery, enchantments,[b] and invocation of saints or other creatures[c] or else risk losing my soul's salvation. Moreover, I should properly acknowledge the only true God,[d] trust in God alone,[e] humbly[f] and patiently[g] expect all good from God alone,[h] and love,[i] fear,[j] and honor[k] God with my whole heart. In short, I would rather reject all creatures than do the least thing contrary to God's will.[l]

a. 1 Cor. 10:5–14. Nevertheless, God was not pleased with most of them, and they were struck down in the wilderness. Now these things occurred as examples for us, so that we might not desire evil as they did. Do not become idolaters as some of them did; as it is written, "The people sat down to eat and drink, and they rose up to play." We must not indulge in sexual immorality as some of them did, and twenty-three thousand fell in a single day. We must not put Christ to the test, as some of them did, and were destroyed by serpents. And do not complain as some of them did, and were destroyed by the destroyer.

These things happened to them to serve as an example, and they were written down to instruct us, on whom the ends of the ages have come. So if you think you are standing, watch out that you do not fall. No testing has overtaken you that is not common to everyone. God is faithful, and he will not let you be tested beyond your strength, but with the testing he will also provide the way out so that you may be able to endure it. Therefore, my dear friends, flee from the worship of idols.

Cf. 1 COR. 6:9–10.

b. LEV. 19:31. Do not turn to mediums or wizards; do not seek them out, to be defiled by them: I am the Lord your God.

Cf. DEUT. 18:10–12.

c. MATT. 4:10. Jesus said to him, "Away with you, Satan! for it is written, 'Worship the Lord your God, and serve only him.'"

Cf. REV. 19:10; 22:8–9.

d. JOHN 17:3. "And this is eternal life, that they may know you, the only true God, and Jesus Christ whom you have sent."

e. JER. 17:5, 7. Thus says the Lord: Cursed are those who trust in mere mortals and make mere flesh their strength, whose hearts turn away from the Lord. . . . Blessed are those who trust in the Lord, whose trust is the Lord.

f. 1 PET. 5:5–6. In the same way, you who are younger must accept the authority of the elders. And all of you must clothe yourselves with humility in your dealings with one another, for "God opposes the proud, but gives grace to the humble." Humble yourselves therefore under the mighty hand of God, so that he may exalt you in due time.

g. HEB. 10:36. For you need endurance, so that when you have done the will of God, you may receive what was promised.

Cf. ROM. 5:3–4; PHIL. 2:14; COL. 1:11–12.

h. JAMES 1:17. Every generous act of giving, with every perfect gift, is from above, coming down from the Father of lights, with whom there is no variation or shadow due to change.

Cf. Ps. 104:27–28.

i. DEUT. 6:5. You shall love the Lord your God with all your heart, and with all your soul, and with all your might.

Cf. MATT. 22:37.

j. DEUT. 6:2. . . . so that you and your children and your children's children may fear the Lord your God all the days of your life, and keep all his decrees and his commandments that I am commanding you, so that your days may be long.

Cf. Ps. 111:10; PROV. 1:7; 9:10; MATT. 10:28.

k. REV. 5:13. Then I heard every creature in heaven and on earth and under the earth and in the sea, and all that is in them, singing, "To the one seated on the throne and to the Lamb be blessing and honor and glory and might forever and ever!"

l. MATT. 10:37. "Whoever loves father or mother more than me is not worthy of me; and whoever loves son or daughter more than me is not worthy of me. . . ."

Cf. MATT. 5:29–30; ACTS 5:29.

What is idolatry?

It is to imagine, cling to, or trust in something other than or in addition to the one true God who has been revealed in God's Word.[a]

a. GAL. 4:8–9. Formerly, when you did not know God, you were enslaved to beings that by nature are not gods. Now, however, that you have come to know God, or rather to be known by God, how can you turn back again to the weak and beggarly elemental spirits? How can you want to be enslaved to them again?

Cf. 1 CHRON. 16:26; 2 CHRON. 15:12; PHIL. 3:18–19; EPH. 2:12; 2 JOHN 1:9.

LORD'S DAY 35

Question 96

What does God require in the second commandment?

That we should not make any image[a] of God or worship God in any other way than God has commanded in God's Word.[b]

a. ACTS 17:29. Since we are God's offspring, we ought not to think that the deity is like gold, or silver, or stone, an image formed by the art and imagination of mortals.

Cf. DEUT. 4:15–19; ISA. 40:18–25; ROM. 1:23.

b. 1 SAM. 15:23. "For rebellion is no less a sin than divination, and stubbornness is like iniquity and idolatry. Because you have rejected the word of the Lord, he has also rejected you from being king."

Cf. DEUT. 12:30–32; MATT. 15:9.

Question 97
Then should we not make any images at all?

God should not and cannot be pictured in any way. As for creatures, even though they may indeed be portrayed, God forbids making or keeping any image of them in order to worship them, or to use them to serve God.[a]

a. EXOD. 23:24; 34:13–14. . . . you shall not bow down to their gods, or worship them, or follow their practices, but you shall utterly demolish them and break their pillars in pieces. . . . You shall tear down their altars, break their pillars, and cut down their sacred poles (for you shall worship no other god, because the Lord, whose name is Jealous, is a jealous God).

Cf. NUM. 33:52; DEUT. 4:15–16; 7:5; 12:3–4; 2 KINGS 18:3–4.

Question 98
But may not pictures be tolerated in churches as books for uneducated people?

No, for we must not try to be wiser than God who does not want to have God's people taught by lifeless idols,[a] but rather by the living preaching of God's Word.[b]

a. HAB. 2:18–20. What use is an idol once its maker has shaped it—a cast image, a teacher of lies? For its maker trusts in what has been made, though the product is only an idol that cannot speak! Alas for you who say to the wood, "Wake up!" to silent stone, "Rouse yourself!" Can it teach? See, it is gold and silver plated, and there is no breath in it at all. But the Lord is in his holy temple; let all the earth keep silence before him!

Cf. Jer. 10:8.

b. 2 Tim. 3:16–17. All scripture is inspired by God and is useful for teaching, for reproof, for correction, and for training in righteousness, so that everyone who belongs to God may be proficient, equipped for every good work.

Cf. 2 Pet. 1:19.

Lord's Day 36

Question 99
What is required in the third commandment?

That we must not profane or abuse the name of God by cursing,[a] by giving false testimony,[b] or by unnecessary oaths.[c] Nor should we participate in such horrible sins of others by our silence or connivance. To summarize, we must use the holy name of God only with fear and reverence[d] so that God may be rightly confessed[e] and worshiped by us[f] and be glorified in all our words and works.[g]

a. Lev. 24:11, 13, 16. The Israelite woman's son blasphemed the Name in a curse. And they brought him to Moses—now his mother's name was Shelomith, daughter of Dibri, of the tribe of Dan—The Lord said to Moses, saying: One who blasphemes the name of the Lord shall be put to death; the whole congregation shall stone the blasphemer. Aliens as well as citizens, when they blaspheme the Name, shall be put to death.

b. Lev. 19:12. And you shall not swear falsely by my name, profaning the name of your God: I am the Lord.

c. Matt. 5:37. "Let your word be 'Yes, Yes' or 'No, No'; anything more than this comes from the evil one."

Cf. JAMES 5:12. Above all, my beloved, do not swear, either by heaven or by earth or by any other oath, but let your "Yes" be yes and your "No" be no, so that you may not fall under condemnation.

d. PS. 99:3. Let them praise your great and awesome name. Holy is he!

DEUT. 28:58–59. If you do not diligently observe all the words of this law that are written in this book, fearing this glorious and awesome name, the Lord your God, then the Lord will overwhelm you and your offspring. . . .

e. MATT. 10:32. "Everyone therefore who acknowledges me before others, I also will acknowledge before my Father in heaven. . . ."

f. 1 TIM. 2:8. I desire, then, that in every place the men should pray, lifting up holy hands without anger or argument. . . .

g. COL. 3:17. And whatever you do, in word or deed, do everything in the name of the Lord Jesus, giving thanks to God the Father through him.

Cf. ROM. 2:24; 1 TIM. 6:1.

Question 100
Then is the profaning of God's name by cursing and swearing so great a sin that God is also angry with those who do not do their utmost to prevent and forbid it?

Indeed yes,[a] for no sin is greater or more provocative to God than the profaning of God's name. Consequently, God commanded it to be punished with death.[b]

a. LEV. 5:1. When any of you sin in that you have heard a public adjuration to testify and—though able to testify as one who has seen or learned of the matter—does not speak up, you are subject to punishment.

b. LEV. 24:15–16. And speak to the people of Israel, saying: Anyone who curses God shall bear the sin. One who blasphemes the name of the Lord shall be put to death; the whole congregation shall stone the blasphemer. Aliens as well as citizens, when they blaspheme the Name, shall be put to death.

LORD'S DAY 37

Question 101
But may we not swear oaths by the name of God in a pious manner?

Yes, when the civil authorities require it of their citizens, or also when it may be necessary to maintain and promote fidelity and truth, to the glory of God and our neighbor's welfare. Such swearing of oaths is grounded in God's Word[a] and therefore has been appropriately done by God's people under the old and new covenants.[b]

a. DEUT. 6:13. The Lord your God you shall fear; him you shall serve, and by his name alone you shall swear.

Cf. DEUT. 10:20; ISA. 48:1; HEB. 6:16.

b. Cf. GEN. 21:24; 31:53–54; JOSH. 9:15, 19; 1 SAM. 24:22; 2 SAM. 3:35; 1 KINGS 1:28–30; ROM. 1:9; 2 COR. 1:23.

Question 102
May we swear by the saints or any other creatures?

No, for a lawful oath involves calling upon God, as the only searcher of hearts, to bear witness to the truth, and to punish me if I swear falsely.[a] No creature is worthy of such honor.[b]

a. 2 COR. 1:23. But I call on God as witness against me: it was to spare you that I did not come again to Corinth.

b. MATT. 5:34–35. "But I say to you, Do not swear at all, either by heaven, for it is the throne of God, or by the earth, for it is his footstool, or by Jerusalem, for it is the city of the great King."

LORD'S DAY 38

Question 103
What does God require in the fourth commandment?

First, that the ministry of the gospel and Christian teaching be maintained,[a] and that I diligently attend church, especially on the Lord's day,[b] to learn the Word of God,[c] to participate in the holy Sacraments,[d] to call publicly upon the Lord,[e] and to give in a Christian way service and resources to the needy.[f] Second, that I will stop doing evil works all the days of my life, allow the Lord to work in me through the Spirit, and so begin in this life the eternal Sabbath.[g]

a. 2 TIM. 2:2; 3:15. . . . and what you have heard from me through many witnesses entrust to faithful people who will be able to teach others as well. . . . and how from childhood you have known the sacred writings that are able to instruct you for salvation through faith in Christ Jesus.

Cf. 1 TIM. 4:13–16; 5:17; 1 COR. 9:13–14.

b. LEV. 23:3. Six days shall work be done; but the seventh day is a sabbath of complete rest, a holy convocation;

you shall do no work: it is a sabbath to the Lord throughout your settlements.

Cf. Ps. 68:26.

c. ROM. 10:17. So faith comes from what is heard, and what
is heard comes through the word of Christ.

I COR. 14:19. . . . nevertheless, in church I would rather
speak five words with my mind, in order to instruct others also, than ten thousand words in a tongue.

Cf. I COR. 14:29, 31.

d. I COR. 11:24. and when he had given thanks, he broke it
and said, "This is my body that is for you. Do this in
remembrance of me."

e. I TIM. 2:1. First of all, then, I urge that supplications,
prayers, intercessions, and thanksgivings be made for
everyone. . . .

f. I COR. 16:2. On the first day of every week, each of you
is to put aside and save whatever extra you earn, so that
collections need not be taken when I come.

g. ISA. 66:23. From new moon to new moon, and from sabbath to sabbath, all flesh shall come to worship before
me, says the Lord.

16. LOVE AND SERVICE OF THE NEIGHBOR—
THE SECOND TABLE OF THE LAW

LORD'S DAY 39

Question 104
What does God require in the fifth commandment?

That I show all honor, love, and faithfulness to my father

and mother and to all who have authority over me; that I submit myself with due obedience to their helpful instruction and discipline,[a] and that I also bear patiently their failings,[b] since it is God's will to govern us by their hands.[c]

a. EPH. 6:1–4. Children, obey your parents in the Lord, for this is right. "Honor your father and mother"—this is the first commandment with a promise: "so that it may be well with you and you may live long on the earth." And, fathers, do not provoke your children to anger, but bring them up in the discipline and instruction of the Lord.

ROM. 13:1–2. Let every person be subject to the governing authorities; for there is no authority except from God, and those authorities that exist have been instituted by God. Therefore whoever resists authority resists what God has appointed, and those who resist will incur judgment.

Cf. PROV. 1:8; 4; 20:20; DEUT. 6:6–9.

b. PROV. 23:22. Listen to your father who begot you, and do not despise your mother when she is old.

1 PET. 2:18. Slaves, accept the authority of your masters with all deference, not only those who are kind and gentle but also those who are harsh.

c. COL. 3:18–21. Wives, be subject to your husbands, as is fitting in the Lord. Husbands, love your wives and never treat them harshly. Children, obey your parents in everything, for this is your acceptable duty in the Lord. Fathers, do not provoke your children, or they may lose heart.

Cf. EPH. 6:1–9; ROM. 13:1–8; MATT. 22:21.

Lord's Day 40

Question 105
What does God require in the sixth commandment?

That I should not revile, hate, injure, or kill my neighbor, either by thought, or word, or look, much less by an action, whether by myself or through another,[a] but put aside all desire for revenge;[b] and furthermore that I do not harm myself or deliberately endanger myself.[c] Therefore the civil authorities are armed with the sword in order to prevent murder.[d]

a. MATT. 5:21–22. "You have heard that it was said to those of ancient times, 'You shall not murder'; and 'whoever murders shall be liable to judgment.' But I say to you that if you are angry with a brother or sister, you will be liable to judgment; and if you insult a brother or sister, you will be liable to the council; and if you say, 'You fool,' you will be liable to the hell of fire."

b. ROM. 12:19. Beloved, never avenge yourselves, but leave room for the wrath of God; for it is written, "Vengeance is mine, I will repay, says the Lord."

Cf. EPH. 4:26; MATT. 5:25, 39–40; 18:35.

c. MATT. 4:7. Jesus said to him, "Again it is written, 'Do not put the Lord your God to the test.'"

d. ROM. 13:4. . . . for it is God's servant for your good. But if you do what is wrong, you should be afraid, for the authority does not bear the sword in vain! It is the servant of God to execute wrath on the wrongdoer.

Cf. GEN. 9:6; MATT. 26:52.

Question 106
But does this commandment speak only of killing?

By forbidding murder God intends to teach us that God hates the root of murder, which is envy,[a] hatred,[b] anger, and the desire for revenge,[c] and that God regards all these as implicit murder.[d]

a. GAL. 5:19–21. Now the works of the flesh are obvious: fornication, impurity, licentiousness, idolatry, sorcery, enmities, strife, jealousy, anger, quarrels, dissensions, factions, envy, drunkenness, carousing, and things like these. I am warning you, as I warned you before: those who do such things will not inherit the kingdom of God.

Cf. ROM. 1:29.

b. 1 JOHN 2:9. Whoever says, "I am in the light," while hating a brother or sister, is still in the darkness.

c. ROM. 12:19. Beloved, never avenge yourselves, but leave room for the wrath of God; for it is written, "Vengeance is mine, I will repay, says the Lord."

d. 1 JOHN 3:15. All who hate a brother or sister are murderers, and you know that murderers do not have eternal life abiding in them.

Question 107
Then is it enough that we do not kill our neighbor in any such ways?

No, for by condemning envy, hatred, and anger, God requires us to love our neighbor as ourselves,[a] to show patience, peace, gentleness,[b] mercy,[c] and kindness[d] toward our neighbor, to prevent harm to our neighbor as much as we can,[e] and also to do good even to our enemies.[f]

a. MATT. 22:39. "And a second is like it: 'You shall love your neighbor as yourself.'"

  MATT. 7:12. "In everything do to others as you would have them do to you; for this is the law and the prophets."

b. ROM. 12:10. . . . love one another with mutual affection; outdo one another in showing honor.

  Cf. EPH. 4:2; GAL. 6:1–2; MATT. 5:5.

c. MATT. 5:7. "Blessed are the merciful, for they will receive mercy."

  Cf. LUKE 6:36.

d. ROM. 12:15–18. Rejoice with those who rejoice, weep with those who weep. Live in harmony with one another; do not be haughty, but associate with the lowly; do not claim to be wiser than you are. Do not repay anyone evil for evil, but take thought for what is noble in the sight of all. If it is possible, so far as it depends on you, live peaceably with all.

e. MATT. 5:45. ". . . so that you may be children of your Father in heaven; for he makes his sun rise on the evil and on the good, and sends rain on the righteous and on the unrighteous."

f. MATT. 5:44. "But I say to you, Love your enemies and pray for those who persecute you. . . ."

  ROM. 12:20–21. No, "if your enemies are hungry, feed them; if they are thirsty, give them something to drink; for by doing this you will heap burning coals on their heads." Do not be overcome by evil, but overcome evil with good.

LORD'S DAY 41

Question 108
What does the seventh commandment teach us?

That all unchastity is condemned by God,[a] and that we should despise it from the heart,[b] and live chastely and modestly,[c] whether in holy marriage or in the single life.[d]

a. GAL. 5:19–21. Now the works of the flesh are obvious: fornication, impurity, licentiousness, idolatry, sorcery, enmities, strife, jealousy, anger, quarrels, dissensions, factions, envy, drunkenness, carousing, and things like these. I am warning you, as I warned you before: those who do such things will not inherit the kingdom of God.

b. JUDE 23. . . . save others by snatching them out of the fire; and have mercy on still others with fear, hating even the tunic defiled by their bodies.

c. 1 THESS. 4:3–4. For this is the will of God, your sanctification: that you abstain from fornication; that each one of you know how to control your own body in holiness and honor. . . .

d. HEB. 13:4. Let marriage be held in honor by all, and let the marriage bed be kept undefiled; for God will judge fornicators and adulterers.

Cf. 1 COR. 7:1–9, 25–28.

Question 109
In this commandment does God forbid nothing more than adultery and similar sins?

Since our body and soul are both temples of the Holy Spirit, it is God's will that we keep both pure and holy.

Therefore God forbids all unchaste actions, gestures, words,[a] thoughts, desires,[b] and whatever may excite people to them.[c]

a. EPH. 5:3–4. But fornication and impurity of any kind, or greed, must not even be mentioned among you, as is proper among saints. Entirely out of place is obscene, silly, and vulgar talk; but instead, let there be thanksgiving.

   Cf. 1 COR. 6:18–20.

b. MATT. 5:27–29. "You have heard that it was said, 'You shall not commit adultery.' But I say to you that everyone who looks at a woman with lust has already committed adultery with her in his heart. If your right eye causes you to sin, tear it out and throw it away; it is better for you to lose one of your members than for your whole body to be thrown into hell."

c. EPH. 5:18. Do not get drunk with wine, for that is debauchery; but be filled with the Spirit. . . .

   Cf. 1 COR. 15:33.

LORD'S DAY 42

Question 110
What does God forbid in the eighth commandment?

God forbids not only the theft and robbery[a] that are punished by the civil authorities, but God also regards as theft all evil tricks and schemes by which we seek to get for ourselves our neighbor's belongings, whether by force or by pretense of fairness,[b] such as phony weights[c] and measures,[d] deceptive merchandising,[e] counterfeit money, excessive interest,[f] or any other means forbidden by God. God also forbids all greed[g] and abuse or waste of God's gifts.

a. 1 COR. 6:10. . . . thieves, the greedy, drunkards, revilers, robbers—none of these will inherit the kingdom of God.

Cf. 1 COR. 5:9–13.

b. LUKE 3:14. Soldiers also asked him, "And we, what should we do?" He said to them, "Do not extort money from anyone by threats or false accusation, and be satisfied with your wages."

Cf. 1 THESS. 4:6.

c. PROV. 11:1. A false balance is an abomination to the Lord, but an accurate weight is his delight.

d. EZEK. 45:10. You shall have honest balances, an honest ephah, and an honest bath.

Cf. DEUT. 25:13–16.

e. PROV. 12:22. Lying lips are an abomination to the Lord, but those who act faithfully are his delight.

f. LUKE 6:35. "But love your enemies, do good, and lend, expecting nothing in return. Your reward will be great, and you will be children of the Most High; for he is kind to the ungrateful and the wicked."

Cf. PS. 15:5.

g. LUKE 12:15. And he said to them, "Take care! Be on your guard against all kinds of greed; for one's life does not consist in the abundance of possessions."

h. LUKE 16:1–2. Then Jesus said to the disciples, "There was a rich man who had a manager, and charges were brought to him that this man was squandering his property. So he summoned him and said to him, 'What is this that I hear about you? Give me an accounting of your management, because you cannot be my manager any longer.'"

Question 111
But what does God require of you in this commandment?

That I promote my neighbor's welfare wherever I can and am able to, treat him as I would have others treat me,[a] and work diligently so that I may be able to help the poor in their need.[b]

a. MATT. 7:12. "In everything do to others as you would have them do to you; for this is the law and the prophets."

b. EPH. 4:28. Thieves must give up stealing; rather let them labor and work honestly with their own hands, so as to have something to share with the needy.

   Cf. PHIL. 2:4.

LORD'S DAY 43

Question 112
What is required in the ninth commandment?

That I do not bear false witness against anyone,[a] distort anyone's words,[b] be a gossip or a slanderer,[c] or condemn anyone rashly or without a hearing.[d] Instead I am required to avoid, under penalty of God's wrath, all lying and deceit as the very works of the devil.[e] In judicial and all other matters I must love, speak, and confess the truth honestly.[f] In fact, I must defend and promote my neighbor's good name as much as I can.[g]

a. PROV. 19:5. A false witness will not go unpunished, and a liar will not escape.

b. Ps. 15:3, 5. . . . who do not slander with their tongue, and do no evil to their friends, nor take up a reproach against their neighbors; . . . who do not lend money at interest, and do not take a bribe against the innocent. Those who do these things shall never be moved.

c. Rom. 1:29–31. They were filled with every kind of wickedness, evil, covetousness, malice. Full of envy, murder, strife, deceit, craftiness, they are gossips, slanderers, God-haters, insolent, haughty, boastful, inventors of evil, rebellious toward parents, foolish, faithless, heartless, ruthless.

d. Matt. 7:1. "Do not judge, so that you may not be judged."

Cf. Luke 6:37.

e. John 8:44. "You are from your father the devil, and you choose to do your father's desires. He was a murderer from the beginning and does not stand in the truth, because there is no truth in him. When he lies, he speaks according to his own nature, for he is a liar and the father of lies."

Prov. 12:22; 13:5. Lying lips are an abomination to the Lord, but those who act faithfully are his delight. The righteous hate falsehood, but the wicked act shamefully and disgracefully.

Cf. Lev. 19:11–12.

f. Eph. 4:25. So then, putting away falsehood, let all of us speak the truth to our neighbors, for we are members of one another.

Cf. 1 Cor. 13:6.

g. 1 Pet. 4:8. Above all, maintain constant love for one another, for love covers a multitude of sins.

17. THE JOY OF THE RIGHTEOUS PERSON

Lord's Day 44

Question 113
What is required in the tenth commandment?

That not even the least inclination or thought contrary to any of God's commandments should ever enter into our heart, but that we should constantly hate all sin with our whole heart and take pleasure in all righteousness.[a]

a. Rom. 7:7. What then should we say? That the law is sin? By no means! Yet, if it had not been for the law, I would not have known sin. I would not have known what it is to covet if the law had not said, "You shall not covet."

Question 114
Can those who are converted to God keep these commandments perfectly?

No, for even the holiest people only make a tiny beginning in holiness in this life.[a] However, with earnest intent they begin to live according to all the commandments of God, and not just some of them.[b]

a. 1 John 1:8. If we say that we have no sin, we deceive ourselves, and the truth is not in us.

Rom. 7:14. For we know that the law is spiritual; but I am of the flesh, sold into slavery under sin.

b. ROM. 7:22–23. For I delight in the law of God in my inmost self, but I see in my members another law at war with the law of my mind. . . .

JAMES 2:10. For whoever keeps the whole law but fails in one point has become accountable for all of it.

Question 115

Then why does God so strictly have the ten commandments preached to us, if no one can keep them in this life?

First, so that all our life long we may become more and more aware of our sinfulness,[a] and therefore seek more fervently the forgiveness of sins and righteousness in Christ.[b] Second, so that we may continuously and eagerly beg God for the grace of the Holy Spirit, so that we may be transformed into the image of God more and more, until we finally achieve full perfection after this life.[c]

a. 1 JOHN 1:9. If we confess our sins, he who is faithful and just will forgive us our sins and cleanse us from all unrighteousness.

Cf. Ps. 32:5; ROM. 3:19; 7:7.

b. ROM. 7:24–25. Wretched man that I am! Who will rescue me from this body of death? Thanks be to God through Jesus Christ our Lord! So then, with my mind I am a slave to the law of God, but with my flesh I am a slave to the law of sin.

c. 1 COR. 9:24. Do you not know that in a race the runners all compete, but only one receives the prize? Run in such a way that you may win it.

Cf. PHIL. 3:12–14.

18. PRAYER

Lord's Day 45

Question 116
Why is prayer necessary for Christians?

Because it is the most important aspect of the gratitude that God requires of us,[a] and because God will give grace and the Holy Spirit only to those who earnestly and unceasingly beseech God and give thanks for these gifts.[b]

a. Ps. 50:14–15. Offer to God a sacrifice of thanksgiving, and pay your vows to the Most High. "Call on me in the day of trouble; I will deliver you, and you shall glorify me."

b. Matt. 7:7–8. "Ask, and it will be given you; search, and you will find; knock, and the door will be opened for you. For everyone who asks receives, and everyone who searches finds, and for everyone who knocks, the door will be opened."

Cf. Luke 11:9–13.

Question 117
What is in a prayer that pleases God and is heard by God?

First, that we earnestly call only upon the one true God who has been revealed to us in God's Word,[a] for everything that God has commanded us to ask of God.[b] Second, that we thoroughly grasp our need and misery[c] so that we may humble ourselves before the face of the divine majesty.[d] Third, that we may be firmly assured[e] that, in spite of our unworthiness, God will certainly hear our prayer for the sake of Christ our Lord, as God has promised in the Word.[f]

a. Ps. 145:18. The Lord is near to all who call on him, to all who call on him in truth.

JOHN 4:24. "God is spirit, and those who worship him must worship in spirit and truth."

b. 1 JOHN 5:14. And this is the boldness we have in him, that if we ask anything according to his will, he hears us.

Cf. JAMES 1:5; ROM. 8:26.

c. ISA. 66:2. All these things my hand has made, and so all these things are mine, says the Lord. But this is the one to whom I will look, to the humble and contrite in spirit, who trembles at my word.

Cf. 2 CHRON. 20:12.

d. 2 CHRON. 7:14. . . . if my people who are called by my name humble themselves, pray, seek my face, and turn from their wicked ways, then I will hear from heaven, and will forgive their sin and heal their land.

e. JAMES 1:6. But ask in faith, never doubting, for the one who doubts is like a wave of the sea, driven and tossed by the wind. . . .

f. MATT. 7:8. "For everyone who asks receives, and everyone who searches finds, and for everyone who knocks, the door will be opened."

JOHN 14:13–14. "I will do whatever you ask in my name, so that the Father may be glorified in the Son. If in my name you ask me for anything, I will do it."

Cf. DAN. 9:17; ROM. 10:13.

Question 118
What has God commanded us to ask of God?

All things necessary for soul and body[a] which Christ the Lord has included in the prayer that he himself taught us.

a. JAMES 1:17. Every generous act of giving, with every perfect gift, is from above, coming down from the Father of lights, with whom there is no variation or shadow due to change.

MATT. 6:33. "But strive first for the kingdom of God and his righteousness, and all these things will be given to you as well."

Question 119
What is the Lord's Prayer?

"Our Father in heaven, hallowed be your name. Your kingdom come, your will be done, on earth as it is in heaven. Give us this day our daily bread, and forgive our debts, as we forgive our debtors; and lead us not into temptation, but deliver us from evil, for yours is the kingdom, and the power, and the glory, forever. Amen.[a]

a. MATT. 6:9–13. "Pray then in this way: Our Father in heaven, hallowed be your name. Your kingdom come. Your will be done, on earth as it is in heaven. Give us this day our daily bread. And forgive us our debts, as we also have forgiven our debtors. And do not bring us to the time of trial, but rescue us from the evil one."

Cf. LUKE 11:2–4.

19. OUR LORD'S SUPPER

LORD'S DAY 46

Question 120
Why has Christ commanded us to address God as "Our Father"?

To awaken in us, at the very beginning of the prayer, the childlike reverence and trust in God that should be the foundation of our prayer, which is the fact that God has become our father through Christ and will much less deny us what we ask God in faith than our human parents will refuse us earthly things.[a]

a. MATT. 7:9–11. "Is there anyone among you who, if your child asks for bread, will give a stone? Or if the child asks for a fish, will give a snake? If you then, who are evil, know how to give good gifts to your children, how much more will your Father in heaven give good things to those who ask him!"
Cf. LUKE 11:11–13.

Question 121
Why is "in heaven" added?

That we may have no earthly concept of the heavenly majesty of God,[a] but that we may expect from God's almighty power all things necessary for body and soul.[b]

a. JER. 23:23–24. Am I a God near by, says the Lord, and not a God far off? Who can hide in secret places so that I cannot see them? says the Lord. Do I not fill heaven and earth? says the Lord.

Cf. ACTS 17:24–25.

b. ROM. 8:32. He who did not withhold his own Son, but gave him up for all of us, will he not with him also give us everything else?

Cf. ROM. 10:12.

LORD'S DAY 47

Question 122

What is the first petition?

"Hallowed be your name." That means: first of all help us to know you truly,[a] and to hallow, glorify, and praise you in all your works, in which your almighty power, wisdom, goodness, justice, mercy and truth shine.[b] We should so order our whole life in thought, word, and deed that your name may never be blasphemed on our account, but may always be honored and praised.[c]

a. JOHN 17:3. "And this is eternal life, that they may know you, the only true God, and Jesus Christ whom you have sent."

Cf. JER. 9:23–24; MATT. 16:17; PS. 119:105; JAMES 1:5.

b. PS. 119:137. You are righteous, O Lord, and your judgments are right.

Cf. ROM. 11:33–36.

c. PS. 71:8. My mouth is filled with your praise, and with your glory all day long.

PS. 115:1. Not to us, O Lord, not to us, but to your name give glory, for the sake of your steadfast love and your faithfulness.

Lord's Day 48

Question 123
What is the second petition?

"Your kingdom come." That is: so govern us by your Word and Spirit that we may always submit ourselves to you more and more.[a] Support and increase the church.[b] Destroy the works of the devil, every power that raises itself against you, and all evil plots thought up against your holy Word,[c] until the full coming of your kingdom[d] when you will be all in all.[e]

a. Matt. 6:33. "But strive first for the kingdom of God and his righteousness, and all these things will be given to you as well."

   Ps. 119:5. O that my ways may be steadfast in keeping your statutes!

b. Ps. 51:18. Do good to Zion in your good pleasure; rebuild the walls of Jerusalem...

c. 1 John 3:8. Everyone who commits sin is a child of the devil; for the devil has been sinning from the beginning. The Son of God was revealed for this purpose, to destroy the works of the devil.

   Cf. Rom. 16:20.

d. Rev. 22:17. The Spirit and the bride say, "Come." And let everyone who hears say, "Come." And let everyone who is thirsty come. Let anyone who wishes take the water of life as a gift.

   Cf. Rom. 8:22–24.

e. 1 Cor. 15:20, 28. But in fact Christ has been raised from the dead, the first fruits of those who have died. When all things are subjected to him, then the Son himself will also be subjected to the one who put all things in subjection under him, so that God may be all in all.

Lord's Day 49

Question 124

What is the third petition?

"Your will be done on earth as it is in heaven." That is: grant that we and all people may surrender our own will[a] and submit ourselves without grumbling[b] to your will which alone is good, so that all people may fulfill their offices and callings as willingly and faithfully[c] as the angels in heaven.[d]

a. MATT. 16:24. Then Jesus told his disciples, "If any want to become my followers, let them deny themselves and take up their cross and follow me."

Cf. TITUS 2:12.

b. LUKE 22:42. "Father, if you are willing, remove this cup from me; yet, not my will but yours be done."

Cf. ROM. 12:2; EPH. 5:10.

c. 1 COR. 7:24. In whatever condition you were called, brothers and sisters, there remain with God.

d. Ps. 103:20. Bless the Lord, O you his angels, you mighty ones who do his bidding, obedient to his spoken word.

Lord's Day 50

Question 125
What is the fourth petition?

"Give us this day our daily bread." That is: provide for all our bodily needs[a] so that by so doing we may know that you are the only source of all good,[b] and that without your blessing neither our solicitude and our labor or your gifts can do us any good.[c] Therefore may we shift our trust away from all creatures and place it in you alone.[d]

a. Ps. 104:27–28. These all look to you to give them their food in due season; when you give to them, they gather it up; when you open your hand, they are filled with good things.

Cf. Matt. 6:25–34.

b. Acts 14:17. ". . . yet he has not left himself without a witness in doing good—giving you rains from heaven and fruitful seasons, and filling you with food and your hearts with joy."

Cf. Acts 17:25.

c. 1 Cor. 15:58. Therefore, my beloved, be steadfast, immovable, always excelling in the work of the Lord, because you know that in the Lord your labor is not in vain.

Cf. Deut. 8:3; Ps. 37:3–11, 16–17; 127:1–2.

d. Ps. 55:22. Cast your burden on the Lord, and he will sustain you; he will never permit the righteous to be moved.

Cf. Ps. 62:8; 146:3.

Lord's Day 51

Question 126

What is the sixth petition?

"And forgive our debts, as we also have forgiven our debtors." That is: for the sake of Christ's blood, do not charge to us miserable sinners our many transgressions, nor the evil which still always clings to us.[a] We also find in ourselves this evidence of your grace, that it is our sincere intention to genuinely forgive our neighbor.[b]

a. 1 John 2:1–2. My little children, I am writing these things to you so that you may not sin. But if anyone does sin, we have an advocate with the Father, Jesus Christ the righteous; and he is the atoning sacrifice for our sins, and not for ours only but also for the sins of the whole world.

Cf. Ps. 51:1–7.

b. Matt. 6:14–15. "For if you forgive others their trespasses, your heavenly Father will also forgive you; but if you do not forgive others, neither will your Father forgive your trespasses."

Lord's Day 52

Question 127

What is the sixth petition?

"And do not bring us to the time of trial, but rescue us from the evil one." That is: since we are so weak that we cannot stand by ourselves for one moment,[a] and since our deadly enemies, the devil,[b] the world,[c] and our own sinfulness[d] constantly assail us, preserve and strengthen us through the power of the Holy Spirit so that we may stand firm against them and not be defeated in this spiritual war,[e] until we gain complete victory at last.[f]

a. JOHN 15:5. "I am the vine, you are the branches. Those who abide in me and I in them bear much fruit, because apart from me you can do nothing."

Cf. PS. 103:14; ROM. 8:26.

b. 1 PET. 5:8. Discipline yourselves, keep alert. Like a roaring lion your adversary the devil prowls around, looking for someone to devour.

c. JOHN 15:19. "If you belonged to the world, the world would love you as its own. Because you do not belong to the world, but I have chosen you out of the world—therefore the world hates you."

Cf. EPH. 6:12.

d. ROM. 7:23. . . . but I see in my members another law at war with the law of my mind, making me captive to the law of sin that dwells in my members.

Cf. GAL. 5:17.

e. MATT. 26:41. "Stay awake and pray that you may not come into the time of trial; the spirit indeed is willing, but the flesh is weak."

Cf. MARK 13:33.

f. 1 THESS. 3:13; 5:23. And may he so strengthen your hearts in holiness that you may be blameless before our God and Father at the coming of our Lord Jesus with all his saints. May the God of peace himself sanctify you entirely; and may your spirit and soul and body be kept sound and blameless at the coming of our Lord Jesus Christ.

Question 128

How do you close this prayer?

"For yours is the kingdom, and the power, and the glory, forever." That is, we ask all this of you because, as our king having power over all things, you are both able and willing to give us all that is good,[a] and that by this your holy name, and we ourselves, may be glorified forever.[b]

a. ROM. 10:12–13. For there is no distinction between Jew and Greek; the same Lord is Lord of all and is generous to all who call on him. For, "Everyone who calls on the name of the Lord shall be saved."

   Cf. 2 PET. 2:9.

b. JOHN 14:13. "I will do whatever you ask in my name, so that the Father may be glorified in the Son."

   Cf. Ps. 115:1.

Question 129

What is the meaning of the little word "Amen"?

"Amen" means: so shall it truly and surely be. For it is much more certain that my prayer is heard by God than I am certain that I do desire these things from God.[a]

a. 2 COR. 1:20. For in him every one of God's promises is a "Yes." For this reason it is through him that we say the "Amen," to the glory of God.
   2 TIM. 2:13. . . . if we are faithless, he remains faithful— for he cannot deny himself.
   ISA. 65:24. Before they call I will answer, while they are yet speaking I will hear.
   Cf. JER. 28:6.

Selected Bibliography

Barth, Karl. *The Heidelberg Catechism for Today*. Translated by
Shirley Guthrie. Richmond, VA: John Knox Press, 1964.

Bierma, Lyle D. *An Introduction to the Heidelberg Catechism:
Sources, History, and Theology*. Grand Rapids: Baker
Academic, 2005.

Bruggink, Donald ed. *Guilt, Grace, and Gratitude*. New York: Half
Moon Press, 1963.

Good, James. *The Heidelberg Catechism in Its Newest Light*.
Philadelphia: The Publication and Sunday School Board of the
Reformed Church in the United States, 1914.

Hoeksema, Herman. *The Triple Knowledge: An Exposition of the
Heidelberg Catechism*. 3 vols. Grand Rapids: Reformed Free
Press, 1972.

Klooster, Fred. *Our Only Comfort: A Comprehensive Commentary
on the Heidelberg Catechism*. 2 vols. Grand Rapids: Faith
Alive, 2001.

Kuyvenhoven, Andrew. *Comfort and Joy: A Study of the
Heidelberg Catechism*. Grand Rapids: Faith Alive, 1988.

Olevianus, Caspar. *A Firm Foundation: An Aid to Interpreting the
Heidelberg Catechism*. Translated and edited by Lyle Bierma.
Grand Rapids: Baker Press, 1995.

Richards, George. *The Heidelberg Catechism: Historical and Doctrinal Studies*. Philadelphia: Publication and Sunday School Board of the Reformed Church in the United States, 1913.

Thompson, Bard, Henrdikus Berkhof, Eduard Schweizer, and Howard Hageman. *Essays on the Heidelberg Catechism*. Philadelphia: United Church Press, 1963.

Ursinus, Zacharias. *The Commentary of Dr. Zacharias Ursinus on the Heidelberg Catechism*. Translated by G. W. Willard. Reprint. Phillipsburg, NJ: P&R Press, 1985.

Verhey, Allen. *Living the Heidelberg: The Heidelberg Catechism and the Moral Life*. Grand Rapids: CRC Publications, 1986.

Visser, Derk. *Controversy and Conciliation: The Reformation and the Palatinate*. Allison Park, PA: Pickwick Publications, 1986.

— — —. *Zacharius Ursinus: Reluctant Reformer, His Life and Times*. New York: United Church Press, 1983.

Williamson, G. I. *The Heidelberg Catechism: A Study Guide*. Phillipsburg, NJ: P&R Publishing, 1993.